The Historian
behind the History

The Historian *behind the* History

Conversations *with* Southern Historians

Edited by
MEGAN L. BEVER &
SCOTT A. SUAREZ

Introduction by GEORGE C. RABLE

THE UNIVERSITY OF ALABAMA PRESS
Tuscaloosa

The University of Alabama Press
Tuscaloosa, Alabama 35487-0380
uapress.ua.edu

Typeface: Caslon

Manufactured in the United States of America
Cover design: Michele Myatt Quinn

∞

The paper on which this book is printed meets the minimum requirements of American National Standard for Information Sciences—Permanence of Paper for Printed Library Materials, ANSI Z39.48-1984.

Cataloging-in-Publication data is available from the Library of Congress.
ISBN: 978-0-8173-1851-2
E-ISBN: 978-0-8173-8784-6

Copyright Information for Interviews

"A Conversation with Dr. William Freehling" was originally published in *Southern Historian* 28 (Spring 2007) by the University of Alabama.

"A Conversation with Laura Edwards" was originally published in *Southern Historian* 33 (Spring 2012) by the University of Alabama.

"A Conversation with Dr. James M. McPherson" was originally published in *Southern Historian* 29 (Spring 2008) by the University of Alabama.

"A Conversation with Dr. Gary W. Gallagher" was originally published in *Southern Historian* 26 (Spring 2005) by the University of Alabama.

"A Conversation with Richard J. M. Blackett" was originally published in *Southern Historian* 35 (Spring 2014) by the University of Alabama.

"A Conversation with J. Mills Thornton" was originally published in *Southern Historian* 34 (Spring 2013) by the University of Alabama.

"A Conversation with Dr. Dan T. Carter" was originally published in *Southern Historian* 27 (Spring 2006) by the University of Alabama.

"A Conversation with Dr. Theodore Rosengarten" was originally published in *Southern Historian* 31 (Spring 2010) by the University of Alabama.

"A Conversation with Dr. Glenda Gilmore" was originally published in *Southern Historian* 30 (Spring 2009) by the University of Alabama.

"A Conversation with Dr. Pete Daniel" was originally published in *Southern Historian* 32 (Spring 2011) by the University of Alabama.

Permissions Information for Photographs

Photograph of Laura Edwards by Duke University Photography.

Photograph of James M. McPherson by David K. Crow.

Photograph of Gary Gallagher by Dan Addison.

Photograph of Glenda Gilmore by Kent Mullikan (National Humanities Center, retired).

Photograph of Pete Daniel by Richard Straus (Smithsonian), No. 2006-3839.

In memory of Christopher Swindle
and in honor of Jonathan Hooks and Christian McWhirter

Contents

Preface

This collection comprises a series of interviews that represent the culmination of nearly a decade of dedication by graduate students at the University of Alabama. In 1980, the Beta-Omicron Chapter of Phi Alpha Theta at the University of Alabama began putting out a biannual publication that has since become the *Southern Historian*, an annual journal that features peer-reviewed articles and book reviews written and edited solely by graduate students across the United States. In 2004 the journal's editors, Jonathan Hooks and Christian McWhirter, envisioned a broader impact for their publication and decided that the *Southern Historian* should embark on a series of interviews with prominent historians. As a young doctoral student, Christian found himself preoccupied with questions that tend to vex most people who pursue a higher degree in the historical field, from the procedural issues such as passing comprehensive examinations and selecting a viable dissertation topic to the more pragmatic concerns of navigating the world of publishing and finding a job in academia.

Christian knew that there were not many good places for graduate students to seek answers to their pressing questions related to the historical profession and decided that the *Southern Historian* could become such a venue. After all, it was a journal created by and for graduate students. With guidance and support from Kari Frederickson, George C. Rable, and Lawrence F. Kohl, all well-respected members of the faculty, the project took off. The first conversation with Gary W. Gallagher was wildly popular, and after that the interview became one of the primary features of the journal. Since 2005, graduate students have continued to engage in conversations with historians who study the American South from diverse perspectives.

The historians featured come from disparate educational backgrounds and study a wide array of topics. Taken together, however, their stories show the importance and vitality of the field of southern history. By casting new light on murky subjects, the historians whose words fill the following pages show that understanding the mysteries of southern history is of vital importance to understanding the history of the United States. This collection contributes to a conversation southern historians have been having about the field for years—a discussion that has been chronicled in collections edited by John B. Boles, Deborah Gray White, Constance B. Schulz, Elizabeth Turner, and others. We hope that the interviews and opinions expressed in *The Historian behind the History* further enrich discussions of southern history, and to that end we have provided a bibliography of supplemental readings we believe will inspire further meaningful conversations among students of the American South—both graduate students learning their craft and seasoned veterans whose passion for their field has endured.

Acknowledgments

This project has taken more than ten years to develop, and we would be remiss if we did not thank the many people who have facilitated the process along the way. The staff at the University of Alabama's Office of Student Media has provided assistance for the *Southern Historian* through the years by guiding graduate students through the process of publishing a journal. From the beginning, they have been supportive of the interview series and have helped us with the recording and the transcribing of the conversations. We would especially like to thank Paul Wright and Traci Mitchell, who are always available to offer suggestions and answer our questions. The faculty of the Department of History has proved an invaluable network of support for this project as well, especially the board of the *Southern Historian*. Kari Frederickson breathed life into the interview project ten years ago when our journal was struggling, and she and George Rable have continued to follow and support the project as the collection flourished. Finally, we would like to thank the University of Alabama Press for enthusiastically supporting this project. After Dan Waterman took an initial interest in the project, Donna Cox Baker helped guide us through the process of publication.

Of course, no part of this collection would have come to fruition without the help of our many historians and their interviewers. To the scholars who have taken time out of their schedules to chat with us over the years, we are grateful for your time and your willingness to share your expertise with us. Likewise, we extend our thanks to more than a dozen of our current and former graduate students who worked on this project while serving on the editorial staff of the journal. We would also like to thank Jonathan Hooks and Jill Cooley, who helped immensely behind the scenes. Another of our colleagues, Christopher Swindle, worked on the project while he was on staff with the *Southern Historian* but passed away before being able to contribute an interview.

Introduction

George C. Rable

For any work of history there are at least two stories: the story told by the historian and historian's own story. Readers naturally focus on the history itself—its argument, structure, evidence, and style—but the historian behind the history also matters and in fact carries considerable interest. The interviews in this book—all conducted by graduate students in the History Department at the University of Alabama—reveal a good deal about the lives (and stories) of some distinguished historians. All those interviewed are in one way or another scholars of the American South, though they have widely varying ideas about how to define and approach that subject. Their personalities and opinions along with diverse philosophies of history and life all shine through in these pages. Their experiences may be atypical in many ways, but even so they are illuminating.

These are all historians who have tackled large subjects and wrestled with big ideas. But they are also human beings whose backgrounds, educations, and careers took many unexpected twists and turns. Theirs are success stories in an overcrowded and highly competitive field, and several acknowledge that fortuitous circumstances and sometimes sheer luck played a significant role in their professional lives.

Some of these scholars were born in the South and were deeply shaped by their experiences. J. Mills Thornton grew up in Montgomery, Alabama, and in many ways (as his scholarship shows), he never really left. South Carolinian Dan T. Carter believes that his early farm work and religious background helped him better understand not only southern history but his students. Several of these historians talk of being shaped by the civil rights movement—in Greensboro, North Carolina, Glenda Gilmore felt like an eyewitness to history. Even Minnesotan James M. McPherson, who studied with the dean of southern historians, C. Vann Woodward, at Johns Hopkins, recalls sit-ins in Baltimore.

Many of these interviews recapture the excitement, uncertainties, and fears of graduate education. Theodore Rosengarten greatly enjoyed his undergraduate and graduate training even though Harvard only reluctantly accepted his study of southern sharecropper and union activist Ned Cobb as a "dissertation." William W. Freehling found much to dislike about graduate school but fell in love with teaching, and a passion for undergraduate education guided his career. Several of these historians admit being unsure about what they were doing in graduate school. Laura Edwards speaks of "feeling" her way along through the program at the University of North Carolina and confessed that she needed a good deal of guidance. Gary W. Gallagher came perilously close to not completing his PhD work at the University of Texas. Richard J. M. Blackett explains how he never managed to earn a doctorate because he never fulfilled the residency requirements at the University of Manchester. He then adds—and others in this group of historians might well agree—that his career was decidedly unplanned. Some of these scholars developed very close relationships with their major professors, others more distant ones. Most express some ambivalence and reservations about graduate education. Several believe that graduate school encourages students to take a hypercritical view of even the best historical works and gives too little attention to teaching history.

Not surprisingly the graduate student interviewers asked some probing questions about the job market and received some strongly worded responses, especially about colleges' and universities' growing reliance on adjunct instructors. In answers sometimes tinged with what could be termed "survivor guilt," several historians admitted how easy it had once been for qualified people to land good jobs coming out of graduate school. As McPherson put it, "I was born of the right gender and race at the right time in American history." The attitudes of these veteran scholars about the current job situation and the near future range from tempered optimism to deep pessimism. They seem to disagree about whether or not there is even a *roughly* functioning meritocracy at work. Most recommend that aspiring historians cast their nets widely and consider the possibilities of public history. Rosengarten and Pete Daniel especially speak of exploring unconventional career paths outside academe.

Many of the conversations focused on the historians' scholarship, but even here the discussions were personal as well as academic. With considerable eloquence and passion, these historians express both their commitment to history and their enthusiasm for studying history. Gilmore talks of examining how people made decisions and their relationship with power. Rosengarten and Edwards emphasize innovative ways to learn about the people left out of conventional histories, while McPherson speaks of viewing history both from the top down and bottom up. For Freehling, large questions about how democracies succeed and fail, along with a newfound interest in contingency and coincidence, drive his scholarship. Blackett talks of the importance of examining the actual historical materials even in the age of digitization and of literally getting one's hands dirty in the archives. Gallagher and Thornton both note the messiness and complexity of the historical record along with the challenges of figuring things out. What readers will find in these pages are active minds still excited about the prospect of discovery but with strong opinions about the profession. Gilmore defends the political engagement of academics while Gallagher rejects what he terms "advocacy scholarship" and an emphasis on historical agency. McPherson sees history as an important way to understand the contemporary world, but Thornton deplores the popular desire for simple answers to complex questions.

Although most historians spend too little time thinking about the audience for their work, several of these scholars address that question with considerable verve. Building on his own wide-ranging work that deployed a variety of materials including oral history and photographs, Daniel calls for a "history without boundaries" including museum exhibits and other forms of history to reach a wider public. McPherson says that scholars need to pay more than "lip service" to addressing an educated public beyond other historians. Freehling and Gallagher both emphasize writing for a popular audience. Blackett points out how humbling it is for historians to find out that their books don't really change the world, but he also points out that more historians need to write with a general audience in mind. In several of the interviews, there is an impatience with academic jargon along with concern about current trends in historical scholarship.

All these perspectives display a diverse and at times diffuse look at the state of American historical scholarship in general and the field of southern history in particular. They present a mixed picture of a still-important field of scholarship in a state of flux, and some might say a state of crisis.

They make fascinating reading for neophytes and veteran scholars alike, but they also provide some raw material for a broader, sociological examination of the historical profession. Such a study would include recent, wrenching changes in the publishing business along with technology's impact on both scholarship and teaching. Future interviews could profitably address the study of history in the age of Facebook and Twitter.

1

Pursuing the Mysteries

A Conversation with William W. Freehling

Christian McWhirter

William W. Freehling grew up in Chicago and graduated from Harvard University in 1958. He received his PhD from the University of California, Berkeley in 1963. He has taught at both Berkeley and Harvard and has held full professorships at the University of Michigan and Johns Hopkins University, as well as endowed chairs at SUNY-Buffalo and the University of Kentucky. He retired from university teaching in 2003, served for nine years as the Senior Fellow at the Virginia Foundation for the Humanities in Charlottesville, and is now an independent scholar, writing in his home study in Fredericksburg, Virginia.

Freehling has spent more than forty years researching the antebellum South, beginning with the publication of *Prelude to Civil War: The Nullification Controversy in South Carolina, 1816–1836* (Oxford University Press, 1985), which won both the Nevins and Bancroft Prizes. His later books, *The South versus the South: How Southern Anti-Confederates Shaped the Course of the Civil War* (Oxford University Press, 2002) and a set of works on secession, *The Road to Disunion, Volume I: Secessionists at Bay, 1776–1854* (Oxford University Press, 1990) and *The Road to Disunion, Volume II: Secessionists Triumphant, 1854–1861* (Oxford University Press, 2007), reinterpret the causes of the Civil War and of Confederate defeat. Freehling has also won the Hodges, Jefferson Davis, and Owsley Prizes. His current projects include a book of essays on the Civil War and a reinterpretation of Abraham Lincoln.

This interview was conducted at the 2006 annual meeting of the Southern Historical Association in Birmingham, Alabama, shortly before *The Road to Disunion, Volume II: Secessionists Triumphant, 1854–1861* appeared. In this conversation, Freehling reflects on his teaching and his research and the pleasure of seeking answers to the puzzles and mysteries of the past.

Let's get into your own undergraduate experience at Harvard a little.

My experience at Harvard was fabulous. I thought it was the greatest place in the world. In a place like that, most of the education is with your peers and not as much with the professors. I had wonderful friends.

I wrote my senior honors thesis under Arthur Schlesinger Jr. I was taken with that man and his conception of history because he wanted to write for the general public and he wanted to be involved in his times. I had a very fleeting relationship with him, but it was enough to see that there was an exciting way of being a historian, of being a public historian and a historian whose books are read. He was an inspirational figure, and still is. I've come to disagree with most of his interpretation of history, but I still strongly agree with his conception of history as a literary art. That's one of the reasons I went to Berkeley—to pursue that kind of history.

When did you decide to become a historian?

I've always been interested in history, but I was long arguing with myself over whether to be a medical doctor or a historian. My final decision about that was delayed until well into my second year at Berkeley, after I had to decide whether to accept an offer from Western Reserve University (not yet called Case Western Reserve University) in Cleveland to pursue a PhD and a medical degree simultaneously.

I really disliked my first year of graduate school at Berkeley. It wasn't any of the things that I loved about history. It was an education in small things: how to footnote, how to read picayune books, and especially how to tear them apart. There were teachers that I thought were too petty, narrow, and confining. It wasn't the history that I'd known as an undergraduate, and I thought the whole profession was probably like that: too claustrophobic, too involved with itself, and not involved in the wider world. I didn't want any part of it.

So after my first year at Berkeley, I decided to enroll in only pre-med courses when I returned in the fall and to apply to medical schools. I marched into Kenneth Stampp's office and told him, and he said, "Well, I think you're making a mistake, but good luck." He added, "There's one more thing you could do for us. You can be one of our teaching fellows in history while enrolled in pre-med courses. . . . I think you'd be good, and we have an extra spot. Would you try it?" I said, "Sure," and I just loved teaching the undergraduates the way I wanted to teach, which was making history more expansive, humanistic, and broad. So toward the end of that second Berkeley year, I quit my pre-med courses, turned down Western Reserve's offer, and happily resolved to pursue a Berkeley history PhD exclusively.

So it was teaching that won you over.

Teaching undergraduates and getting away from that graduate education. I've never really gotten past that moment. I've always preferred to teach undergraduates. I've always felt that if I had to teach graduate students, it was going to be in a very different way and in a department that had a very different conception of graduate education. I think that even more strongly now.

What exactly was it about the program at Berkeley that made you feel that it wasn't what you wanted?

It was mostly my research seminar, where we convened as the editorial board of the *American Historical Review*. Every class was on how to write a good article. All the emphasis was on how to write footnotes, how to take notes, and how to protect yourself and write an essay that will further your career. It was so narrow; it took the heart out of the big things that I wanted to know about history.

And then there were the core requirements: you had to learn Spanish, you had to study a field outside of your own whether you were interested in it or not, and there was too much reading. I couldn't possibly read everything and absorb it, so I started to follow some of the tricks that graduate students from time immemorial have been doing just to get through the reading list: reading the preface, reading the conclusion, and reading book reviews. And there was almost no emphasis on writing. There was no emphasis on how you tell a story, how you make history alive, or how you appeal to your fellow citizens as opposed to your fellow academics. It wasn't training me for the kind of career that I wanted, and if that was professional history, I didn't want any part of it.

And that's why you were more drawn to teaching.

I was teaching the big things about history that I love: is history inevitable? What does history say about whether democracies work? How much of a part does contingency play? How much do deep and personal forces play a part? How is it related to the lives that you and I lead? And I was teaching really bright undergraduates. I had special seminars for them after class, and it was just the way it had been my senior year at Harvard. We talked a lot about writing—how you write a story. I was back with why history mattered to me. It was wonderful.

What won you back to the research side of history?

I think it was Kenneth Stampp's attitude. He was my thesis director. I'd gone to Berkeley to study with him because I'd first encountered him back at Harvard when he came as a visiting professor. His attitude was, "Look, I think I know how to be a historian, but I want you to learn to be a historian in your own way. I'm never going to tell you that I would have done it differently. I'm just going to read your chapters with a very light hand and tell you if I think you're doing it well your way. I'll probably end up disagreeing entirely with your dissertation and I don't care. I'm not trying to develop a Stampp school of history; I just want you to do your thing your way." So, I could write history the way I had wanted to as an undergraduate. It was thrilling to try to write a good narrative history just like my mentors back at Harvard had done and have a very thorough professional like Stampp think that's fine.

What drew you to the Nullification Controversy as a dissertation topic?

The romantic version is that I read all of the books on nullification and I thought that they were missing something. They all said that South Carolina was going through this economic crisis, that there was a severe depression, that the planters responded to that depression by trying to knock down the tariff rates, and that they were frustrated by their inability to get a lower tariff by Andrew Jackson, so they developed this scheme of nullifying.

I took the broadest possible look at South Carolina society, and I realized that this was true for only half of the state. It was only true of the Upcountry planters who had worn out their land and were in some kind of economic trouble. It wasn't true at all of the Lowcountry aristocrats, who were primarily growing rice and were not in economic trouble but were leading this nullification campaign. That fascinated me, and none of these books on the tariff as the source of the nullification controversy addressed what caused South Carolinians to get so uptight about all this and bring the nation to the verge of civil war, despite the fact that they were very prosperous. It was an intellectual puzzle.

I still think my initial fascination had very little to do with my life in politics or my life with Arthur Schlesinger Jr. or anything like that. That's probably naive—people don't just live in a vacuum and are motivated by an intellectual puzzle they find, but I still believe that I was. And history is an intellectual puzzle still, and that absolutely fascinates me. It also absolutely fascinates my students. Not history as something they memorize but history as a puzzle in which, if the current interpretation doesn't make sense, you have to go to the sources to try to find out what in the world is going on.

Would you recommend teaching as part of graduate school?

Absolutely. I think every graduate student needs an experience in teaching undergraduates and some counseling and mentoring on how you best do it. There are two things that most professional historians do: they write and they teach. Most graduate schools pay no attention to either one of those things.

It's shocking that some graduate schools don't let students teach. I don't know what they think they're training the people to do. Senior graduate students should teach their own course under very careful mentoring. Teaching, like writing, is something you're either born to do or you're not. There are limits to what you can learn to do in both of these cases, but there's an awful lot you can learn about teaching and an awful lot you can learn about writing. Graduate students could do little things that the department can't otherwise do, like give little seminars for the best students.

I've always thought that one of the most important things to do in undergraduate teaching is to seize the best students and to give them a really exciting conception of what history can do. Not that most of them are going to be historians, because they're not, but there are things that historians do that are very valuable for whatever you do—including and especially writing.

How exactly do you draw them out?

First, like all people, they respond to an interest in them. I try to find them very early and tell them that I'm excited by their work, and would they like to do a little more. Sometimes seizing on the right people is a little difficult to do, because occasionally you'll have a very fine student that doesn't like to talk, and you don't know about that one until they write their first paper. I also believe in extracurricular stuff. Whenever I teach, I always hand out cookies, and I always make sure that they're the best of cookies. I take kids to historical movies, we go to historical sites, and I have lunch with them.

There has to be a personal element to it. That helps you get to the point I want to get to, where you can be very severe. You want to worm your way inside as a teacher and get their affections, so that you can be strict, so that you can be rigid, so that you can say, "You know, I think that this paragraph is terrible and you need to take it home and rewrite it," but you can't do that until you've first gotten them on your side.

That's how I think every teacher should be. I think a lot of people aren't even aware of it and are a little scornful of it. They think that, in a way, it's pandering, and it is if it leads to nothing but a soft kind of education, but if it leads to a really rigorous and critical education, then I think it's great. Be a glad-hander on the one hand and a remorseless critic on the other. If I had been involved in graduate education more than I was, that's how I would have tried to approach it. I would have tried to have been the friend of my graduate students, but I would have been very strict, too.

The one problem that I had with teaching was that I never could find a way to connect my research with my teaching. On the contrary: they were frustrating each other. I was always such a passionately involved teacher and such a passionately involved writer that I had a lot of trouble doing them both at the same time. I had to decide earlier than most people that, if I was going to ever finish my books, I had to get out of teaching. There's a myth that teaching and writing are mutually supportive, but I haven't found that.

Writing was just too complicated, and I'd lose my train of thought, which is why I've published kind of slowly. That's one reason why things have been much better for me as a writer in the four years since I quit teaching.

I'm curious about how you approach surveys.

I try not to teach surveys, but when I do them, I never use a textbook—students hate reading them. And you don't want them to hate what you've assigned. All these multiteam textbooks are not done successfully as a literary exercise—as a way to make history seem like a story, exciting and integrated. I don't care if everybody learns every fact because what used to be considered the facts are no longer the facts. There used to be a canon of academic history. There used to be certain things you had to learn. Now, of course, that's exploded, and most people don't even think that's part of history—that political stuff. So you couldn't possibly get people to memorize all of history anyway anymore, and thank goodness, because memorizing is not the way to make history enjoyable. So that's what I don't do: I don't assign textbooks and I don't expect people to memorize all kinds of facts.

What I do, as much as I can, is I get people to read primary sources and try to have exciting discussions of those sources: like the Lincoln-Douglas debates, like the Georgia secession debates, like the debates between the Federalists and the Anti-Federalists. I like to assign Tocqueville, I like to assign Calhoun, and I like to assign *Uncle Tom's Cabin* in the survey courses, just to give people a taste of how exciting it is to come into contact with documents, to see their mysteries, and to move on from there. The minute you look at the Lincoln-Douglas debates, you see a mystery there—Lincoln is not who you think he is and that intrigues kids. So if they read a textbook, they're not going to get intrigued and they're not going to see history as a puzzle and a mystery.

I once had my graduate students make up their own seminar and they made up a great course of primary readings. They chose the primary readings themselves and we had wonderful discussions of those primary sources. Again, with the Lincoln-Douglas debates, rather than having them read one of the thousands of books on Lincoln, have them read the actual debates to get their engines going. The ultimate point of being a historian is how you handle primary sources—what you squeeze out of the most meaningful primary sources—and there's too little of that in early graduate school. That was, by far, the best graduate seminar I ever taught, and it was partly because they devised it.

I think students will always get more excited when they can devise their own education, but it was also because we got away from "What's wrong with this narrow monograph on this narrow subject?" You get so sick of that. Not "What can be really exciting about this field?" or "What new questions can we raise?" To me, one of the most exciting books that I've ever read is a book that I thoroughly disagree with: Stanley Elkins's *Slavery*.[1] Elkins argues that slaves were "Sambos" and also that there was a real parallel between the experience of slavery and the experience of the concentration camps. I think that's dead wrong, but it's an exciting book because it raises so many really interesting questions. It's full of history as a mystery and how difficult it is to solve that mystery, even if you think his solution is off. So, a book talking just about how Elkins is being absurd about this comparison doesn't make any sense; it's not the way to teach things. The way to think about it is to say, "This guy's got a very interesting question here and even if I don't like his solution, what might the solution be? What kind of research might get me closer to it?" Those are the kinds of books that, if read the right way and discussed the right way, can lead to excitement in graduate school.

Do you feel that graduate seminars focus too heavily on taking apart books?

They do, and it's not fun to read a book to figure out what's wrong with it. It's more fun to read a book expecting that you're going to learn something. You need a sense that the author might not necessarily have all of the answers, but that he or she can teach you something about being a historian, and there's too little of that in graduate school.

It's just too much reading. You just can't read six hundred pages a week in each of your courses with an eye to finding out what the mysteries are. There's this constant overconcentration of reading so graduate students don't have any choice but to cut corners instead of getting involved in the romance and excitement of history.

Did you do much graduate teaching during your career?

Not very much. I directed eight PhD students who I inherited from Willie Lee Rose at Johns Hopkins. Willie Lee had had an absolutely marvelous career, and she attracted a series of really superb graduate students to Hopkins, and I was their second reader. That was a role I liked because I wasn't responsible for their education but I could participate in it. She had this terrible stroke, and I inherited all of her graduate students. All those I saw to completion. Outside of that, I've only had one graduate student who went all the way to his PhD, and I was reluctant to take that one student on. I'm delighted that I did, but he has had a struggle. Part of my reluctance about teaching graduate students is my feeling about this difficult job market.

I was going to ask you about that.

To some extent, you're preparing people to break their hearts. I had this experience when I was handling one of Willie's students. His name was Larry Shore, and he did a very good book on the economics of slavery after the Civil War. He was in serious contention for prizes and he's a really sharp guy but he couldn't get a job anywhere in America, no matter what I did—no matter what he did. He ended up at Queens University in Canada. After about four or five years, he was totally frustrated and I was totally frustrated, so he quit his job and went to law school and since has been very prosperous as a lawyer, but it broke his heart. So I watched this happen, and I've also watched it happen with a favorite nephew of mine, who got a wonderful PhD at the University of Texas and never could get an academic job. He finally became a curator at the Smithsonian and has thrived at that.

There's been one exception [to Freehling's tendency not to advise graduate students]. When I worked briefly at SUNY-Buffalo, there was one student who really stood out and was really exciting and he just begged me to take him on. He thrived in graduate school. He wrote a wonderful book, but then he struggled to get a job and finally got a job at a technical school in New York, which he is not satisfied with. I find this very difficult—to help people become exciting historians and then watch them get so frustrated.

It's going to get better—I've been saying that for twenty years. The reason it doesn't get better is because of these damned deans, who really are a menace in the academic world. They're trying to run a capitalistic enterprise, and they can get these adjunct professors. What is the word for it—scab labor. These deans can hire these people for very little money. They can ask them to teach one course, so that people teach about five courses in a metropolitan area by rotating around schools. They get no benefits, no assurance of employment, no spousal consideration, and no medical care. It's very cheap, and the deans get very good people who are desperate. If I could abolish one thing in my profession, it's those adjunct professors because it gives deans an out from hiring the best people coming out of graduate school. Even the best people, these days, usually have to serve an apprenticeship of three or four years in these adjunct positions. The only way you can justify it is as a capitalist—not as an educator, not as an academic, not as someone who loves to see young people thrive.

What do you think changed in the profession?

That's a fabulous question. I've puzzled about it so often because, on the one hand, universities are richer than ever—they have incredible resources that they didn't have back in the 1950s and 1960s. On the other hand, they're broke and they're relying on all of these economic gimmicks, like adjunct professors. Why is there this economic crisis at a time when endowments are booming? Some of it, I'm sure, had to do with technology and with the huge new expenses that the computer revolution brought. Some of it has to do with affirmative action and the huge new expenses that open the university to everyone. I firmly believe in that. Those two things didn't much exist in the 1950s and are a big part of most universities' budgets, but I don't think that's enough to explain it.

It's odd because all academics seem to know there's a problem and seem to be bothered by it, but the system continues to perpetuate itself.

And that's what's happening: the *system* is perpetuating itself. The deans are happy with the solutions they've made, but what caused the problem? How did the universities get broke at a time when they've never been so rich? No one's ever explained it to me to my satisfaction. Why is there greater poverty in a time of much greater abundance?

Would you discourage undergraduates from entering graduate school?

I warn them and warn them. I tell them, "If you have to do it—do it. It's the greatest life in the world and I wouldn't have had anything else for myself, but be aware of the pitfalls." I would add, "Be sure you train yourself to do something else besides academic history if you need to." There are many other exciting ways to practice history. The profession is almost completely unaware of them and has almost no training for them.

Everyone should have at least one course in being a curator: of exhibits, of battlefields, and so forth. I think that's where most of the history education is going on these days. Everybody should take at least one course in TV and radio because there's a wonderful future there. Everybody should get a lot of training in writing because there are a lot of jobs in the government and out of the government for historical writers.

What's happening in the profession is that people are being trained for this very narrow range of jobs, which is getting narrower and more frustrating all of the time, and there's this other world out there to which the graduate schools pay little attention. Places like George Mason, and especially the University of South Carolina, are aware of this and are doing a wonderful job of reconceptualizing what graduate education is all about. If I really wanted to be at the center of graduate education, I would be at a school like that and I would be pushing it like hell.

It sounds like all of this revolves around the question of what people think historians ought to be doing. Many of the jobs you've talked about wouldn't cross some historians' minds because they have no interest in educating the general public.

There's a very claustrophobic view of what historians do in a public democracy. Whether the graduate schools prepare for it or not, there are these very important roles that historians play. One of those is writing for the general public, and I think it's scandalous that historians don't try to write the kinds of books that journalists write.

Didn't that used to be the case?

You bet. When I was growing up in the profession, all of the most outstanding historians were writing for the general public: Richard Hofstadter, David Potter, Arthur Schlesinger Jr., Daniel Boorstin—they were all best-selling writers.

They all knew how to tell a story. They all knew how to write language that had nice short sentences, no long words, but still was very sophisticated and very cultivated, and nobody was more sophisticated and cultivated than Richard Hofstadter. They had a different conception: they saw themselves as public historians as well as academics. We've lost that, and I think we've got to get it back.

How do you feel about graduate exams?

I'm not too sure why we do exams, but if we must keep them, I think it should be a matter of asking people to read some books and some source materials and making some sense out of those. It never bothered me for somebody to say, "You know, I haven't read that book," or "I only had a chance to read half of that book." The only thing I was concerned about was what you made of the books you had read. If you hadn't made anything of them and found nothing interesting, then I think you're in the wrong business.

The way I always handled reading lists for fields is I would say, "I want you to create your own field and to select your own books and I want at least a third of them to be primary sources, but if they are all primary sources, that's great. And I want you to devise your written question—I might add a wrinkle to it—but you'll know exactly what you're going to write about. And I want you to be creative with your answer."

What I was looking for was a creative approach to the reading that had been done and an excitement about pursuing the mysteries.

Would you throw out the orals?

I think the orals are more fun. The big thing is to try to make it a fun conversation, to make an exam to determine how a young person is beginning to approach the mysteries. I can see a point to it, if you do that. If they have to take a PhD exam, I'd like to see them take an outside field if it's a field that they think might be of use to them someday. The whole point of it should be to make history seem alive and exciting in all kinds of ways. The very best people come out of the process with that sense, but for most people, it's a drag, which is a shame because it is good fun.

In some ways it seems like you're always fighting in graduate school to maintain your initial passion for history, because the process is very hard on it.

I think one of the ways you could better sustain graduate students would be to show them examples of how they could make it interesting, and that means learning how to curate shows because millions of people go through these museums and present a real opportunity for education. And millions of people pick up these magazines and documentaries on history, and if you could find some way to let graduate students know that there are all these other ways to get at the mysteries of history and to get other people interested in them besides the monographic way, I think it would sustain that excitement. That's why they enter graduate school, and then they find this other world, like I did.

Tell me about your brief time teaching at Harvard after you finished at Berkeley.

I went back to Harvard for a year, and I was put in the most piddling kind of position, as junior people were at Harvard in those days. There was absolutely no American historian who had risen in the ranks at Harvard. Finally, Bernard Bailyn did, and he was the last person until very recently. I was not getting the kind of freedom I had enjoyed at Berkeley. After about six weeks I had decided that my mecca, Harvard, wasn't such a mecca.

A lot of really wonderful junior people at Harvard went through that same kind of experience, and I became very close friends with them, especially George Frederickson, who didn't find it as narrowing as I did. I think there was some kind of prejudice at Harvard against people coming back with a PhD from somewhere else, whereas George had gone right through at Harvard and knew all about it. He had a somewhat more liberal kind of conception of his role there.

You also taught at the University of South Carolina.

I taught at South Carolina before I went to Harvard. I had gone to South Carolina to research my dissertation, and I was eating peanut butter sandwiches. I went to the head of the South Carolina History Department—Robert Ochs—and asked him if I could possibly teach. I told him I'd teach anything. He said, "Well, how about teaching night school?" I said, "Sure. Who are my students going to be?" He said, "Mostly, troops at Fort Jackson," and they were the most exciting students I've ever had. It wasn't going to fly to teach them the seven causes of the French Revolution; they were only interested in history as mystery, history as story, history as contingency, and they were just wonderful students.

That story says a lot about the changes in the job market. You could never go to a department today and just ask for a job.

No, I was so lucky. After I published *Prelude to Civil War*, I had a choice of six different departments willing to give me tenure right away as a beginning assistant professor. No matter how good you are, you can't do that now. Back then graduate school was based on the notion that everybody would be lucky—that everybody who got a PhD would get a job, would get tenure. And then the world changed but graduate schools didn't.

Why have you moved around to so many different universities during your career?

In some ways I wish I hadn't because the best place that I ever taught at was the University of Michigan. That was a wonderful school for me for all kinds of reasons, but I left and I went to Hopkins; Hopkins was just not the right place for me. It was a school that relied entirely on graduate education for its sense of purpose and undergraduates were sort of an afterthought, and they were my babies. Other professors at Hopkins were perfectly glad to have one professor be interested in undergraduates, but I was working in isolation with very few other people sharing that passion, and ultimately I decided that I had to get back to a school like Michigan where I'd once again be part of a whole group of people who were teaching undergraduates enthusiastically.

I went to SUNY-Buffalo, and that was the wrong place for me, too. Then I went off to Kentucky, which was absolutely the right place for me. It wasn't as intellectually exciting as Michigan because Michigan, back in those days, was just tremendous. We had an incredible department: John Higham, Gordon Wood, Jack Greene, and Brad Perkins. It was a wonderful place.

I was struck by how much you moved around, since settling in to one institution for the duration of one's career was seemingly the normal process until rather recently.

And I lost something because of that. For example, my friend Leon Litwack is just now retiring from Berkeley, and he's been teaching there for thirty or forty years. He's an institution there, and everybody loves him. That's a wonderful life to lead, and I wish I had had that kind of life. It should have been back at Michigan. Michigan was a wonderful place—still is—but it didn't work out that way.

You've probably been asked this before, but since you're from Chicago, went to school in the West, and taught in the North, do you feel that you're somehow less equipped to do southern history, as some have suggested?

That's the one thing that I can't tolerate: the assumption that we can't understand some people unless we are one of those people ourselves—that men can't understand women; that parents can't understand children; that blacks can't understand whites. To me it denies what history is all about, which is learning through the sources to see somebody else's world their way. The only review of my work that I've ever objected to was one that ended by saying, in effect, "The trouble with this book is that this is a Yankee writing about the South and no northerner can do this successfully." That really annoyed me, and I've never since really felt the same way about the person who wrote that.

I think it's wrong about the human mind, it's wrong about marriages, it's wrong about parenting, and it's wrong about teaching. It's wrong to suggest that we can't understand our students just because we're not twenty anymore. There are some things we can't understand, but there's a lot that we can understand if we talk to them and listen to them. Human beings can't connect or be involved with each other if empathy is impossible. I really do think that, as an outsider, I can get inside southern people's heads as well as a southerner can. I can go on forever, because that assumption really makes me mad.

They say that no northerner can write southern history, but many of these southerners are men. By their rationale, how are they supposed to understand southern women? If they're white, how are they supposed to understand southern blacks? They're free capitalists—how are they supposed to understand the slaveholder mentality? It's not as if they are what they are studying, which is southerners in the past. I just think that whole way of thinking has got to be fought every inch of the way.

History is a lesson in forgetting yourself as much as you possibly can and empathizing with people very different from you in the past. I don't know if it helps me or hurts me to be a northerner, but I think it's absurd to say that someone from Chicago can't understand Charleston.

I became a southern historian because I don't find the North as mysterious or as puzzling. I see the North before the Civil War as a much more understandable society and not doing some of the crazy things that southerners were doing. There's a very good English historian named John Ashworth, who has written a really interesting critique of my work in which he says you can't write about the coming of the Civil War unless you write about the North. I suppose there's some truth in that, but I see the northern response to the South as a very simple mystery—one that's easily unlocked. I don't find that with the South. I think what the South ended up doing is very weird, exotic, and mysterious, and that's what attracts me—puzzles.

You've written before about how growing up in the aftermath of World War II and the collapse of democracy in Germany influenced your interest in history. Can you talk about that a little bit?

Sure. That seemed to me to be the most interesting question of all. Back at Harvard, Arthur Schlesinger Jr. wrote an article in the *Partisan Review* that I couldn't agree with. It was an attempt to get rid of the revisionist notion that a group of blunderers had caused the Civil War and replace it with the notion that it had been a straight-out fight between the abolitionists in the North and the slaveholders in the South, but I couldn't see the North as an abolitionist society, partly because of my Chicago background. Chicago's gone a long way toward cleaning itself up in the years since, but it was a pretty vicious culture at that time—a very segregated culture with lots of race riots. I just knew, in my bones, that you could not paint this wonderful North against the South. The more I read the sources, the more I was convinced that racism was very strong in the North, the abolitionists were relatively weak, and Lincoln himself was no abolitionist at the beginning of the war.

That was part of it, and the other part was the great question at that point, and still is for Americans: can democracy endure, is democracy the best system, and can we export democracy to the rest of the world? All of those things were very exciting questions in the 1950s when we were fighting the Cold War and remain very exciting questions. I thought the way to study that question was to study Hitler and Weimar Germany. That was right after World War II, I was well aware of the Holocaust, and I was very aware that Germans *voted* to put Hitler in power. How could that have possibly happened? That's what I really wanted to study, but I couldn't learn the languages. That's one thing that I'm completely intellectually incapable of doing, learning languages.

So I was thrown back to finding another way to study how democracies fail and, to me, that's the story of the coming of the Civil War and the inability of a democracy to peacefully solve the problem of slavery. I don't know if it was a good substitute, but it was a substitute for the original question I had in mind. How did the Weimar Republic destroy itself became how did the North American republic destroy itself.

Or almost destroy itself.

Well, I think it did destroy itself, if you think the way that republics endure is peacefully following processes. The only reason this republic survived is that the North had a stronger army, which is no recommendation of democracy. When I asked that question—"Why did the American democracy destroy itself?"—the imposing parts of the question to me were the southern questions because I saw the mainstream North as constantly reacting to what the South was up to in a defensive way, reacting against what the North thought was the Slave Power. It became important to me to discover why the South was reacting in these powerful ways that caused counterreactions in the North. That's why I became more interested in southern history.

The really mysterious part of that story is how the South ever took the stands that it did until it seceded, despite the fact that most southerners wanted no part of disunion. If you wanted to save slavery the worst way to do it was to fight a civil war against the North. There were Unionists in the South saying this all the time, that it was suicidal and the secessionists would destroy themselves, and the secessionists did.

There is definitely a theme through all of your work of this divided South, and there are some who disagree with you. Are the two volumes of **Road to Disunion** *intended to be your definitive statement on that issue?*

I don't know if anything is ever definitive, but I'm positive that some people will not like certain aspects of my interpretation and that over the years even better books will be written. I have no hope of permanently solving anything, but I do hope to establish that there is a permanent mystery there. I'm very excited that people like Lacy Ford, who is a brilliant historian and much younger than I am, is seeing things that way and is going to write his next book on this divided South. But in terms of whether the South was divided or not, so much depends on how you define the South.

Bill Cooper, for example—who is a good friend of mine and whose work I love—gets around all of the problems that I talked about by only dealing with the parts of the South that seceded. For him, the Border South is not part of the South, and if you look at it that way, a lot of what I have to say becomes silly. But that isn't the way that people were looking at it at the time. The secessionists were desperate about what was going on in the Border South, and they had every right to be, I think. So, as is often so true of history, it's a matter of definition.

I don't think that the planter class was very divided, although there are differences between the planters in various places. I don't think the Black Belt South was very divided, but there are differences between the various Black Belts. But I do think there were big differences between the Black Belt South and the White Belt South. I know that the term "White Belt South" is my invention, but I think it's the right invention: it's the South that had very little slavery, very few blacks. If you want to call those people part of the South, I don't see how you can help but think that it was a divided culture.

This is an argument that's been going on since the war—the secessionists were worried about it, Lincoln was worried about it.

It's even more than that—Lincoln was partly elected by it. The most fascinating thing that I've discovered over the past few years was that it was southerners who put Lincoln over the top in the Republican Convention of 1860. It's the Missouri and Maryland delegations who swung to Lincoln and gave him his necessary majority, and those are exactly the people that the secessionists were worried about: they were in the Republican Party, they were going to get patronage from Lincoln, they were itching to start a debate in the South about whether slavery is right, and the secessionists wanted no part of that debate in the Border South.

So you've got to consider those people southern because the secessionists did and saw the southern Republicans deserting over to Lincoln, to some extent. The fear was that more would desert when he started handing out patronage. Lincoln had a built-in Border South Republican Party if he wanted to seize on it, and he did—very shrewd politics. You could be antislavery and do nothing about it except appoint the right southern people to southern office.

From reading the introduction to the second volume of **Road to Disunion,** *you seem to be downplaying the more common notion that westward expansion caused the Civil War. Am I right?*

It's more that I downplay those forces at the moment of secession and that's because I feel that the actions of South Carolina were absolutely crucial, in terms of having a secession movement and a civil war at that moment. That does not mean that there was never going to be a secession movement had South Carolina not taken the stance it did, but I think for the revolution to start at that point in the way it did with the ultimate result that it did, South Carolina was very crucial. South Carolinians only thought of expansion as a threat to them because it was going to continue the depopulation of South Carolina, and South Carolina was going to continue to lose influence. These South Carolinians were suffering from a very severe decline in influence from the days of Calhoun, and they really haven't been crucial in the national story ever since Calhoun died, with the one exception of Preston Brooks. And it's not an exception that they love.

The world out there was moving away from South Carolina, the American democratic system was moving away from South Carolina, the world out in the West was moving away from them, and they were not that interested in annexing more western territory that would draw more South Carolinian whites and blacks away. So in some ways their secession was a reaction against expansion. They were not interested in the territorial controversy, and they had absolutely no interest in the Crittenden Compromise because it was the wrong issue. So that's what I mean by downplaying it: it's not that I don't think that it's an important issue, but if you want to see how the movement actually began, you have to begin with South Carolina.

That's why they had to work so hard to get the other states in line.

You bet, and that's such an important statement: they had to work so hard. It is hard work carrying out secession, and it's fascinating that they succeeded and how they succeeded. That's the mystery.

So you put the whole thing at the feet of South Carolina?

Well, they started it, and once they started it there was a snowball effect that's very interesting. It didn't really have to be that way except that Buchanan almost immediately decided to send the *Star of the West* down there, and I think that changed the issue. The issue became not "Is it expedient for us to secede?" because the South was very divided on that subject but "Can we bear Yankees firing guns at us and taking away our right to consent to government?"

I think if Buchanan had waited, there might have been a slightly different twist to how the secession story unfolded, but the minute he sent that ship he caused the other Lower South governors in the other six states to seize the forts in their states and create a military crisis before the decision about secession had ever been made in their states.

And that informs the question of why so many southerners fought but saw they weren't fighting for slavery.

Exactly. They were defending their right to withdraw consent and only a slave doesn't have the right to withdraw consent—only a slave can be ruled without his own consent. They felt that they had withdrawn their consent and Lincoln had coerced them. I think that issue became the issue that made secession spread. There was not a successful secession movement in the Upper South, where two-thirds of all southerners lived, until that happened. In that sense, this whole doubt that slavery caused the Civil War has its point, because I don't think most of these guys in Virginia went to war to save slavery. I think most of them went to war in Virginia to prevent themselves from being enslaved by Lincoln's armies.

I think it's safe to say that Road to Disunion, *like secession, snowballed a little since you originally only intended to write a sequel to* Prelude.

There were certainly things that I couldn't understand with the secession crisis and there became more and more things that I didn't understand as I looked, so I kept going further and further back. It was the right way to go about it, but it was an exhausting way. I don't think that I solved everything, and I don't think that it's necessarily going to last, but I do hope that people see that there is a problem with explaining secession, and that history is about problem solving, and it's about explaining exciting people and writing about them and painting them, and finding and writing about exciting places and painting them. I hope that conception lasts even if my answers don't.

The topic also deserves a lot of attention because you don't get a much bigger question in American history. In some ways it's central to the whole American experience.

I think it's central, and it was important for me to pick the central thing. That was the problem way back in that Berkeley seminar: nothing seemed to be important; nothing was at the center of things. If history is going to be exciting, it has to be at the center of things. Graduate schools have to understand that and aging professors have to understand that.

What subjects in southern history are more intriguing to you now and which would you encourage graduate students to go after?

In terms of the material that I've just dealt with, the thing that I'm least satisfied with in my own work is work on the Unionists because it's very obvious to me that they were very bad campaigners. There were several points at which I think they could have been much more effective. I don't think I do a very good job of explaining that poverty of imagination among the Unionists, and I think a terrific book can be written on Unionism.

Another terrific book that I think can be written is on paternalism. What are we going to do with the concept of paternalism? Is paternalism peculiar to slavery, or is it a more general American phenomenon? Somebody has to write a book on slaveholder paternalism versus boardinghouse paternalism in the North in places like the Lowell Mill versus the paternalism of northerners with their house servants, which I witnessed in Chicago in the 1950s. Another slice of the story is the paternalism of graduate student mentors toward students. To me, paternalism seems to be a much more universal American institution than we've made it, and I think somebody's going to write a terrific book on paternalism and if anything is unique about slaveholder paternalism—what is it?

We've talked a little about this already, but I'd like you to describe what role you think history ought to have in American society.

This is a democratic culture, and one of the things that you and I and everybody ought to do is to think about that democratic culture and how to preserve it and how to strengthen it and how to look out for its pitfalls. I think that the story of the coming of the Civil War is very instructive for what can go wrong with a democratic system. For example, one of the things that I think goes very wrong in the South is the intolerance for contrary opinion—an immediately instinctive growl that means that anybody who criticizes slavery in the slightest way is disloyal and must be shut out as a traitor. That's a very important trend in the South, and it's a very important way that the secessionists secure their victory. It's a very dangerous tendency in democracy to think that the opposition is disloyal, and the minute a society gives into that, it verges on becoming undemocratic. I think you see it in the Old South and, alas, I think you've seen it in American politics ever since. I think that the American public has to be aware that that's a dangerous thing to do, and history can teach that.

I also think that the coming of the Civil War can tell people that democracy is a wonderful but problematic institution that doesn't always work and that sometimes collapses. If we have this sense that we're dealing with something fragile, something sensitive, and something that is not universally wonderful, maybe we won't keep going on all these crusades to try to spread this wonderful stuff all over the world. I think that's important. If Americans are constantly aware that their democratic system has had its troubles, they're not going to be so inclined to spread this cure everywhere. That's the kind of thing I mean when I say that history needs to be written for more than professors.

But Americans have always thought that way—they've always had this obsession with the perfection of their society.

And always thinking that in democracy, they have something perfect. Of course, they don't partly because nothing perfect exists and everything in life requires struggle. We need to teach people that there aren't easy answers and that democracy doesn't always work and it's particularly difficult for a democracy to work when you have a dictatorial social system in the middle of it that distrusts contrary opinion. So I just think it's important that we try, at least, to get the people beyond our own academy to see these things.

NOTE

1. Stanley Elkins, *Slavery: A Problem in American Institutional and Intellectual Life* (Chicago: University of Chicago Press, 1959).

2

Reframing Narratives

A Conversation with Laura F. Edwards

Megan L. Bever

After growing up in Connecticut and Tennessee, Laura Edwards completed her undergraduate degree at Northwestern University (1985) and received her MA (1987) and PhD (1991) from the University of North Carolina at Chapel Hill, where she worked with Jacquelyn Dowd Hall and Peter Coclanis. Now a professor of history at Duke University, Edwards is the author of numerous articles and *Gendered Strife and Confusion: The Political Culture of Reconstruction* (University of Illinois Press, 1997), *Scarlett Doesn't Live Here*

Anymore: Southern Women in the Civil War Era (University of Illinois Press, 2000), and, most recently, *The People and Their Peace: Legal Culture and the Transformation of Inequality in the Post-Revolutionary South* (University of North Carolina Press, 2009). She is the recipient of the Southern Historical Association's 2010 Charles Sydnor Award and the American Historical Association's 2009 Littleton-Griswold Prize, as well as a Rockefeller Foundation Fellowship at the National Humanities Center in Research Triangle Park, North Carolina (2007–8), a Mellon Postdoctoral Fellowship in the Humanities at the Newberry Library in Chicago, and a John Simon Guggenheim Fellowship for the 2012–13 academic year. She also received the 2013 Dean's Award for Excellence in Mentoring from the Graduate School at Duke University. She has served as president of the Southern Association for Women Historians and on the board of directors for the American Society for Legal History, and she currently serves on the executive board of the Southern Historical Association.

After delivering the keynote address for the 23rd Annual Southern Intellectual History Circle in February 2011, Edwards was interviewed about her career. In the conversation, she speaks of delving further and further into the past to uncover the legal and political lives of ordinary southerners.

I'd like to start out with your background. You mentioned earlier today that, at first, you wanted to be a musician.

Yes.

Can you explain a little bit why?

Well, we moved when I was in fifth grade from Connecticut to Tennessee, and when we did that, I was playing clarinet. (Beware: This is a long story!) In Connecticut, we started band in fourth grade. They didn't start until fifth grade in Tennessee. So I was a year ahead of everybody, and the music director suggested that I switch to oboe, which I did. And I loved it, so I started taking lessons and became very serious about the oboe.

When I was about fourteen or fifteen, I heard about Interlochen Arts Academy and the North Carolina School of the Arts, which are boarding schools for students interested in the arts. I thought, "I could apply." Of course, I didn't know how to apply or even how to find the addresses of these places, so (improbably) I looked in the back of *American Girl* magazine for advertisements. I couldn't find one for North Carolina School of the Arts, but I found one for Interlochen Arts Academy, and I applied. The teacher of my teacher had just become the first-chair oboist in the New

York Philharmonic, I had had a lesson with him, and he knew the teacher at Interlochen. So by way of this very small network, I got into Interlochen Arts Academy. Of course, I had filled out the application in pencil on my bed, and I had neglected to discuss it with my parents, so they got the letter saying, "Congratulations! Your daughter got into Interlochen Arts Academy." And they were surprised, to say the least. But ultimately I ended up there, and I loved it. I had every intention of being a professional musician, and this seemed like the route to get there. In fact, I lived and breathed music all through high school, and that set the course of where I ultimately ended up, even though I didn't become a professional musician. I even met my husband through music, at Sewanee Summer Music Center when I was sixteen. He was—and is—a trombone player.

Music is what got me interested in history. When I was at Interlochen, I started taking classes in history from teachers there who were not teaching the regular high school curriculum. They were ABDs, who had finished everything but their dissertation, and ended up teaching at Interlochen rather than going into academia. They taught high school classes like college-level classes, and I thought the subject and the approach were completely fascinating. So I started pouring more and more time into history rather than music. Ultimately I decided that I wanted to do history instead of music. So I transferred the focus and work ethic from one to the other: you practice constantly, you learn the literature, and with that background you learn to write history yourself. And so at seventeen years old, I knew that I really wanted to be a historian.

But I had no idea what that entailed or what that meant. It didn't occur to me that you would have to go to graduate school, and the idea of getting a job was not on my radar screen at seventeen. As an undergraduate at Northwestern, I started asking questions about these practicalities. But I felt my way through that whole process.

That sense of feeling my way through the professional standards didn't stop when I was in graduate school. It was surprising to me, for instance, to find out that you were supposed to give papers at conferences. I don't think I had fully grasped that you would have to teach at the college level. I think it sunk in at one point, but it was a novel idea: "Oh, I have to teach a class? Really? My gosh." But I was willing to do what needed to be done to be a historian.

I want to flesh this out a little bit if I can. You made the decision a bit early, but do you remember a moment when you really started looking at grad school seriously or was it just a process that you worked through?

Well, I remember the first moment when I knew that I really wanted to be a *historian*. I didn't have that same feeling about grad school, because the goal was to be a historian, not go to graduate school. I didn't really know what grad school was until later in college, so I couldn't conceive of it before that. Wanting to be a historian was different and more immediate. I was seventeen, and we were writing about the bank crisis, nullification, and presidency of Andrew Jackson in my US history course. We were talking about the political and personal aspects of that conflict, and I was fascinated that the dynamics of the past were so complicated—such a human drama. We were supposed to write a paper based on our readings of various primary and secondary sources on this issue.

It all seems pretty odd now that it was Andrew Jackson's presidency that got me interested in history, but it occurred to me at that moment that whole assignment was about imagining what the past was about. It was in our hands to shape that moment, and I thought, "Wow, that's an incredible power that you would have as a historian." It's not just making pretty music; it actually has implications. And I knew that I wanted to do this kind of storytelling, where you're actually recovering the past, for the rest of my life.

Since I knew so clearly what I wanted to do, I looked for ways to make it happen, and I discovered in college that graduate school was the way to get there. I didn't know how to apply to graduate school or if I could afford to go, so I wasn't sure that I could even think about this as an option at first. It was one of my favorite professors, Carl Smith, who brought up the subject with me and explained the process. That conversation was when I found out that there was funding available to graduate students. Funding was the key issue for me. I did not think that I could go to graduate school if I had to come up with the money to pay for all those years that it would take to earn a PhD. Without help, I didn't see how I was going to be able to make graduate school work financially. And I remember being amazed that schools would pay your tuition and give you a stipend for expenses. I remember walking home from that meeting, clutching my books, thinking, "I can actually do this. This is possible for me to do." That was really exciting.

What made you decide to study southern history specifically?

When we moved from Connecticut to Tennessee, I knew we were moving to the South, but I didn't really know what that meant. I had a real sense of culture shock. It occurred to me at that moment that there are differences in different regions of the country. I couldn't articulate the idea well, but the fact of regional difference was very clear to me

It was also clear that being from eastern Tennessee was not something that you bragged about—that there were negative associations attached to the area. That became obvious when I went to Interlochen, which is in Michigan. In Michigan, when I said that I was from eastern Tennessee, people would stare at me and say: "And you play *oboe*? How did *that* happen?" It was very strange to have all the negative associations of the South, and specifically an area of the South associated with the *Beverly Hillbillies*, get loaded onto you simply because of the geographic place that your parents happened to land. I was less upset or offended than I was interested, though.

At Northwestern I took a freshman seminar in southern history, and I was completely blown away by this class. We started out with U. B. Phillips—and we read the whole book, cover to cover. We went on from there to go through the historiography on slavery. I was stunned by how the past changed depending on how you told it. I was also stunned at slavery because it struck me as such an incredible contradiction in the context of a country supposedly built on ideas of equality and freedom. I thought that if you could explain slavery, then you could get a better handle on a lot of the problems in the United States. It struck me that the South was a really interesting place. Out of all the places you could study in America, it was truly and profoundly the most dramatic and fascinating.

Now, your first book is on Reconstruction and the second on the Civil War. So at some point during your undergraduate years, were you drawn to the Civil War era or how did you end up at that particular—

Moment?

Yes.

Well, I went to graduate school wanting to do twentieth-century US history, specifically the civil rights movement. One of my first courses was an oral history course with Jacquelyn Hall. I loved the course, but I had a hard time interviewing people. The final assignment was based on interviews, but I kept putting them off, although I eventually did do them. I constructed an MA thesis, later, around an oral history project on the civil rights movement. But I kept putting the interviews off again. Instead, I went to the archives to do background research. I kept working my way back in time and eventually ended up in the Reconstruction period—and I had yet to interview anybody.

None of my research had anything to do with my stated project. I remember a frantic call to Jacquelyn Hall, when I said, "I think I've changed my topic. Is this a problem?" She said, "No, it's not a problem, that's fine." But I wasn't changing my topic so much as refining it. I was interested in Reconstruction for the same reasons that I was interested in the civil rights movement. I saw it as a moment in time that made it possible to understand issues of inequality in the United States.

I want to keep talking about southern history but broaden this out just a little bit. What do you think are the benefits of studying the South?

It is the place where I think the most central dynamics in US history are enacted in the most dramatic way. You get US history in broad strokes in the South. To come to grips with US history, you really have to come to grips with southern history, and if you don't, then you're missing the boat, essentially. I think that the implications of southern history are profound, and the payoff in exploring them is profound. Too often we cordon off the South as something different from the rest of the United States, but I'm interested in the region because it is about the rest of the United States. Even when I was first thinking about doing southern history as a freshman in college, what drew me to the region was how all the issues there were about the American experience.

Do you think there are any limitations that southern historians face, either with their scholarship or in the world of American history or in academia?

Yes. In other fields, southern historians can be marginal—they are the outliers who do a distinctly different "southern" version of the topic. So in legal history, a field with which I also identify, historians who work on the South do southern legal history, which encompasses topics unique to the region, such as slavery and race relations. The South does not represent trends in legal history more generally, even though it seems obvious that slavery and race are issues that are central to US history, not just southern history. Still, given the existing presumptions, it's difficult to walk into a field like that and say, "Okay, I'm looking at the South. You all need to listen to me." They're thinking: "Why do we need to listen to you unless we're interested in the South?" I think the key is removing intellectual barriers that characterize the South as a unique place and then having conversations between southern historians and historians in other subfields about what US history really is. Who and what represent US history and why?

That said, southern history has been very influential in defining US history. If you look at the presidents of the Organization of American Historians and the presidents of the Southern Historical Association, there is a lot of overlap. If you go down the list of Organization of American Historian presidents, many of them have done southern history in some form or another. So even as southern history is seen, in some ways, as marginal, the field has been profoundly important in shaping general narratives in US history, which gets back to the reason why I was interested in the field in the first place.

It's a contradiction. Southern history plays a key role in defining narratives in US history, even though southern historians are still pushed to the margins in some fields. I think it says a lot about how we're still grappling with the central issues in southern history, particularly the legacy of slavery, in this country. Even as we're addressing the issue, it can be easier to turn that legacy into a "southern" rather than an "American" problem.

Do you think it's the same reason, perhaps, that the South is sort of marginalized or romanticized in American culture? It just carries over?

I think so. On the one hand, the South is conceived of as distinctive, and so a lot of the discourse within the profession is about this place, "the South." For instance, when I was first hired at Duke, southern history was not seen positively. The sense among some people in the department—although not all—was that it was regional and narrow, and they would then mark the department as a second-tier department with a regional specialization. They wanted to be a history department with a national reputation, which meant emphasizing things other than southern history.

So when I interviewed for the women's history position there, I spent most of my time explaining that although I focused on the South, I was actually interested in broad themes in US history. But, you know, when push comes to shove, the scholarship that many historians—US and otherwise—find interesting is in the field of southern history.

I'd like to talk about your work specifically. I want to talk about your newest book, which has been very well received. You focus on legal history at the local level in the South in the Early Republic. So this time period, again—it's a bit different than even what you did earlier. You're continuing to move backward. What led you back to the Early Republic from Reconstruction?

I think it's the same answer as to how I ended up in Reconstruction as opposed to the civil rights movement. There was a lot that I was taking for granted in the Reconstruction book, and I was interested in exploring what happened before that period. You always have to start someplace, obviously, in your scholarship, and you take the work of other people as foundational, you accept those conclusions, and then you frame your topic based on what's already been done.

But that means you assume a lot about the earlier time period, which—in turn—shapes your own work. So I was interested in seeing how the issues that I explored in Reconstruction got set up. And I was particularly interested in the actions of ordinary African Americans during Reconstruction, particularly the assertiveness of their legal and political actions. The scholarship examines such actions but has not really explained the dynamics behind them. How does a formerly enslaved population get so politically savvy and legally savvy so very quickly? How do they know how to frame issues in ways that clearly resonate with the existing political culture? It struck me as a really interesting thing that we take this transition for granted: "Of course when enslaved people become free, they will drop all their reservations about the legal and political system that kept them in bondage and embrace it as full members of the American public." That assumption is all the more interesting considering the emphasis in the historiography on a separate slave community with a distinct set of cultural values. So if the slave community was separate and different, how is it that enslaved people were able to integrate themselves so easily into all of the major legal and political discourses of the nation once slavery collapsed? It seemed like an interesting transition. I thought that exploring the earlier period might help me understand it.

I was also dissatisfied with the narratives of women's history, which tend to center on the acquisition of rights. Southern women—white and black—tend to drop out of the historiography until late in the suffrage movement, when southern women became active in the movement. There is also the related presumption that the possession of rights is necessary in order to act politically and legally. And it just struck me as problematic to assume that women were not engaged in public issues—issues that involved them, their families, and their communities—until they acquired rights. In fact, other strands of the historiography suggest otherwise.

So I wanted to explore the first half of the nineteenth century, a period when so many southerners didn't have rights and when we think they were not legally or politically engaged—and couldn't be, even if they had wanted to be. Essentially, I wanted to do a political history of those people who were formally excluded from politics and see where that would take me. It's a very different perspective on politics than if you look at the issue assuming that there is some predetermined realm that is, inherently, political and that some people have access—because they possess rights—and that others do not—because they do not possess rights. If you think of politics that way, then you often end up with a history focused on how those who were excluded from that political realm ultimately acquire access to it.

You've reframed the story, it shifts the focus to people who lived in a period in which they never acquired rights and were not involved—and couldn't be involved—in any sort of organization or movement to obtain rights. Then you ask: "How does political history look from that perspective?"

You've mentioned already that your research always focuses on marginalized groups, whether it be white women, African Americans—all of your books do this. Do you think there are particular difficulties writing the history of women or writing the history of enslaved people?

Yes. When I was in graduate school, I would explain that I was considering the connections between the social changes of emancipation and the political issues of Reconstruction. I would explain that I wanted to focus on the changes in the lives of ordinary people, particularly poor whites, African Americans, and all women. The response would often be, "But you can't find anything on those people." Of course that's not the case—there is a ton of material. The problem was that the existing historiographical frameworks, at that time, did not focus on those kinds of people. The problem was our assumptions about what the history of that period was about, not the presence or absence of archival sources.

The local court records are filled with African American men, women, and poor white men. The cases are, primarily, about labor conflicts and social conflicts. The problem was that historians didn't have a framework to connect the issues in those court cases to the central themes in Reconstruction history. And at that point, the historiography still pretty much focused on party politics. Eric Foner's book came out while I was in graduate school.[1] Although the book combined social and political history, the book's structure is conceived primarily through party politics, with the analysis of social change always separate from, although running alongside of, the analysis of political change.

Since then, I think that the scholarship has come a long way in merging social and political history—in understanding how labor issues were political issues, how the process of defining freedom extended in African Americans' daily lives, and how reconstructing southern households was about the reconfiguration of political power. It was less a matter of new research than a matter of reframing the historiographical narratives so that we can make connections that we didn't see before.

To get back to your question, this issue of reframing historiographical narratives is why I'm interested in marginalized people. We've told history from this perspective where we've placed people without formal political power on the margins of our historical narratives. Even in histories that are critical of people's lack of power, there is still an assumption that the lack of power actually does make these people historically marginal in the sense that they could not be active participants because of their political marginality. So we end up writing histories about how marginalized people acquire the rights that will enable them to be central and not marginal—and that essentially frames our narratives around assumed historical actors, namely free white men who had the full range of civil and political rights and who could, as a result, engage actively in the political realm. Throughout US history, that standard represented a minority of people, and yet we've taken this standard as if it were—or should have been—the majority experience. It's not, and it never was, especially in the early nineteenth century. In fact, this standard excludes the vast majority of the population in the United States at this time.

Why do we tell US history in terms of a minority? Why do we tell it as if the minority could stand in for the general experience? That doesn't make any sense. So for me, telling the story of marginalized people is not just about recovering their lives but also about telling the story of an American experience that actually is representative. For me, focusing on women, for instance, would make more sense in terms of creating a representative narrative. We should be generalizing from women's experiences because women's circumstances—in terms of legal and political rights—were actually more like those of most men, who also experienced limitations on their civil and political rights—if they had them at all, which was not the case for many men. The minority of white men with full civil and political rights doesn't even represent most men.

I think we need to recover information on marginalized people, but then you need to go that step further and use their lives to reframe our historical narratives more generally. That's been the goal in my books—to reframe that narrative to tell the story of US history from the majority experience. That makes everything look different.

And where do you think this discussion is going in the future?

I think we'll keep having a discussion about what constitutes the American experience. I'm obviously not the only person who's focused on marginalized people or who is thinking about reframing our historical narra tives in those terms. There's a lot of work out there that does that now. But as a profession, historians move in halting, often partial, steps. I look at my book on Reconstruction, for instance, and there's a lot I would do differently in writing about that topic now. There are things that I think I just got wrong. If I could have read my third book before I did my first book, my first book would be a lot better.

So it's a continual process of thinking and learning. It's a process, not a definitive goal. Ultimately the act of rethinking our historical narratives opens up new questions, which lead to more rethinking. That is exactly what I thought was interesting about history when I was in high school. There are so many stories to tell about the past that are meaningful.

I'm going to keep going on this line but transition just a little bit. I want to talk about your middle book, the synthesis on southern women in the Civil War. And I want to pull something from your introduction because you mention that scholars, of course, have taken notice of marginalized groups, which we've just talked about. But you said that the subject of covering marginalized people hasn't really trickled down—at least not into the classroom. And this was in your introduction of the second book, which was published about ten years ago. Do you think this is still the case or is it getting better?

I think it's getting better, actually. I do. Although it can be hard to tell, because I don't take other people's classes. But you generally get a sense of these things, I think, reading textbooks, although even that is not necessarily representative. I think my main problem is that people without formal power in their historical context are always portrayed as marginal in our historical narratives because of that fact. So we tend to duplicate—often without meaning to—the power relations of the past in our own historical narratives. I try to uncouple those two issues—power relations in the past and how we now write about historical change. The way I tell southern history, for instance, is that southern women—black, white, rich, poor, whatever—have always been very much involved in shaping their society.

I think that one of our problems is that we've been looking in certain places—such as state and national politics—that have been central to the historiography but that tend to exclude women. If you look in those arenas, then you'll inevitably conclude that women were not important. But in the early nineteenth century, the state and national levels of government weren't very active in defining questions about public order in ways that would affect the lives of most women or actually most people. The issue that got me interested in history—the national bank in the Jacksonian period—is exemplary. Questions about the bank were central to party politics at the national level. Ultimately the banking issue did send the country into recession—which did affect people, but the issues were not framed in those terms because no one really foresaw that outcome. Rather, the way in which people talked about the bank at the time involved issues that did not directly impact most people's lives.

Then we look at state-level government and discover—oh, women weren't there, either. But that shouldn't be surprising either, because state governments didn't do that much in the way of public governance. State legislatures met a month out of the entire year and primarily passed private laws. Most of the legislation did not deal with the major issues in people's lives.

In the early nineteenth century, the questions about how you construct your local community (who does what, who behaves how to whom) were far more central in people's lives than the issues dealt with in party politics at the state and national levels. And when you look there, at the level of local government, you see that women were very active and very vocal. And you get a very different image of women. In the historiography, we have a particular view of women's marginality that comes from our focus on certain areas—primarily state and national governments. In those arenas, women were absent or silent because that's the way those levels operated.

But that wasn't the case at the local level, where women were visible and active. So you can retell that story to highlight that women did contribute substantively to questions regarding the shape of their society—if you change the places where you look for those dynamics. If you do, then what happens later in the nineteenth and twentieth centuries makes a lot more sense as well. The women's rights movement didn't come out of nowhere. It actually built on a long tradition of civic engagement. As questions about governing the social order moved from local arenas to state and national governments, women tried to gain access to those spaces. But women's rights, then, was not a huge leap that was unconnected to the past. It was rooted in a past in which women were always central.

And it seems to make more sense to me that way. Instead of a history of marginalized people trying to get admittance to society, you have a history about a range of people who have always informed and shaped historical dynamics and whom we need to take into account. We need to be aware of all of them and their full actions in that society rather than framing a narrative where people's lack of formal power translates into historical marginality.

I think we're making slow progress there, and I don't know that my vision of how to address the issue is the only—or even the best—solution. But I think we need to be more creative in thinking about how to understand people's direct contributions and actions in society while still also being able to deal with the fact that they were subordinate. I think we trip up by assuming that if we emphasize people's active contributions to historical dynamics, then we're somehow denying the hard, often brutal conditions of subordination. It's a really tricky thing, I think, to deal with.

How do we fix this is in, say, a survey course where most college students get their only taste of history? How do we reorganize it?

We quit doing a US history survey course at Duke, so I haven't had the chance to do a survey class in a while; but I do teach the legal history class, which moves from the colonial period to the present in one semester and duplicates a survey in that sense. It also has the same challenges as a US history survey, in the sense that legal history is usually told as top-down narrative, without much attention to ordinary people.

Narratives in legal history tend to focus on the development of law and policy at the state and national levels. You rarely ever see women or African American men except in relationship to slavery, the civil rights movement, or suffrage. I move away from the framework by making the development of legal and government institutions central to the course and questioning what we know about them. I point out that state and national governments grew in power and scope over time. Until they did, most law and policy were done in other places. As a result, it's impossible to focus the course on state and national law—because those areas of law did not deal with most legal issues for much of US history. Those issues were handled elsewhere—often in arenas to which ordinary people had access and in ways where ordinary people could have a say. That is quite different than the usual presumption, which is that a range of issues—health, social welfare, economic regulation, for instance—were handled privately by individuals, and not in law and public policy, until the state or national governments began to address them. And then the question is: how do all these legal issues move into the purview of state and national governments and what does that transition mean?

In the Anglo-American legal tradition, "the people" and "the public interest" are central. So I frame the course around those basic questions: Who are the people? What is the public interest? What legal conflicts do those questions produce? Those legal questions are not necessarily about who had civil and political rights, although that certainly is the case. They're also about conflicts among people *regardless* of their civil and political rights. In fact, rights are not the only means for resolving disputes or determining policy in American history. Is the public interest served, for instance, by supporting the interests of farmers or those of manufacturers? The people, moreover, can include those who don't have civil and political rights, so that questions about preserving the public health of the population more generally can take precedence over the interests of a few individuals. Framing the issues in this way encourages students to think about the privileges and limits of rights-bearing individuals. They're forced to go beyond the legal status of individuals—to go beyond the notion that rights, alone, can solve everything. They also have to come to grips with the fact that very few people even had the full range of civil and political rights. Most important, they also then have to think about the meaning of rights and the changes over time. A lot of free white men had rights in the early nineteenth century, but the array of rights at their disposal was limited compared to what it is in the twentieth century. And the meaning of those rights—what they could accomplish—was also different.

Problematizing the institutional history helps a lot in creating a framework where it's possible to talk about women, African Americans, and ordinary people of all kinds in legal history, because it moves the focus away from the paradigmatic rights-bearing individual. In some ways, I do more with the institutions than I do with people. But it's the institutional analysis that makes it possible to open up the law in ways that allow you to see a wider range of people. So ironically, I walked into legal history thinking that I needed to focus more on African American men, all women, and the poor, and to find out more about their lives, and actually what I needed to do was to find out more about legal and political structures that I assumed we already knew everything about. Now I focus there in order to make ordinary people more visible.

Sometimes I get a little worried when I'm rattling on about the US Constitution and its amendments in a lecture. I think: "How did I get here?" But you have to do that if you're going to remake historical narratives in order to make a wider range of people visible. I think that's where women's historians and African American historians have missed the boat, in some ways—by abandoning the study of government institutions to the political historians and legal historians.

Right, everything has to come together. Now, I know you teach a lot of legal history, and you've also mentioned that you teach a Cold War class or have taught a Cold War class?

I have, indeed.

So I have a very broad question: what's your approach to teaching in general?

I had to think about this recently because I was asked to do a feminist pedagogy seminar. My first response was, "I don't know that I do feminist pedagogy." They said, "Oh, no, you do." I was surprised. "I do? Well, let me think about what I actually do in class."

At the undergraduate level, the lectures provide the narrative line for the class. I don't really depend a lot on a textbook. Instead I have the students read primary source documents. So in legal history class, it's legal documents, but I also use a lot of other material, including images, in my lectures.

I try to incorporate popular culture into the courses as well to make the historical issues more accessible. Legal history tends to be much more focused on formal legal documents for obvious reasons. But in that class, we discuss *To Kill a Mockingbird* as a story about the legal system, rather than just a story about race relations in the South. In my women's history class, we use a wider range of materials. We read memoirs. We read *The Contrast*, which is a play from the post-Revolutionary period. We consider the film *The Graduate* as a document about the complications of feminism in the postfeminist age. We end the course with the film *Fatal Attraction*. We also read novels. We do a range of things.

I'm trying to get the students to think critically about different kinds of sources and how to use them. But I also try to use sources that are both compelling and evocative of time period. The idea is if you give students a novel, they can link it up to the issues we talked about in the lectures but in a way that allows them to talk freely about those ideas and to explore them. If you can start with the characters or plot in a novel or film, they can work through the issues within that context and, from there, move to the broader historical themes.

So that's the general approach. The Cold War class was fun that way because I taught the course with a friend in the English Department, Priscilla Wald. When we were putting the course together, we started out with the texts from the period, rather than thinking in terms of chronology and historical issues, as historians usually do. In talking about the texts—films, novels, images, plays—we worked through the historical context that would best help the students understand the material. So we would say, "Okay, here's the movie we want to use. What are the historical themes that come out of this movie?" Which is completely backward from the way I would usually put together a course. Usually I would identify historical issues or events and then go find primary materials to help students understand those issues or events. We used a wide range of materials. We used films. We did a whole section on the *Andy Griffith Show* as a way to understand the reaction to consumerism in the Cold War period. We used instructional films that they show in school about dating dos and don'ts, personal grooming, and other issues. We would mix things up, so that Priscilla would do the Beat poets and I would follow up the next day with Andy Griffith. It was an interesting class that way. It was also a lot of fun because the students were using the actual primary materials, thinking through the historical issues themselves, and playing with those ideas.

This is something I've noticed a bit, and again, I've worked primarily as a TA, but I've noticed that the twentieth-century historians get to do this a lot, and it's a little bit harder when teaching the first half of American history.

Yes.

So how do we do this? How do we make our students engage with early US history if that's what we're teaching?

It's harder. I've started using more images because you can get great images from the eighteenth and nineteenth centuries now from various websites. One really good way to illustrate the connection between conceptions of gender and colonization is to show maps, which tend to depict the land as a natural, untamed space (gendered female) that is being civilized by Europeans (gendered male). There's this one image in particular of Savannah, Georgia. Savannah is depicted a rectangle of civilization cut out of nature. There are little rows of streets and houses, with boats in the harbor, and then the vast, untamed wilderness behind it.

You can use that map in a lecture that lays out conceptions of gender in early modern Europe. Women, then, were being associated with different characteristics than they are today. They lacked self-control (like nature), and they needed to be subordinate and tamed. They were considered to be closer to nature, more emotional, and less rational. Then you show the maps, and the students say, "Oh, I see." And they can: they can actually see a very abstract concept.

I also try to find court cases that would tell them a story, and there are lots of those. There's one from colonial North Carolina involving a woman named Dorothy Steele, who ran away with two men, one of whom is clearly her lover. Along the way, they were helped out by slaves who had the kind of autonomy not usually associated with slavery—and that's only one among many of the interesting components of the case. The whole incident raises all kinds of questions about slavery and the position of free white women. Why did she run away? What did she want to happen? Ultimately the man she runs away with is prosecuted for rape. She is not prosecuted for anything at all, even though she was the one who was masterminding the whole thing.

In discussing this case, students have to come to terms with women's subordination but also the fact that women had power. The way Dorothy Steele appears in the legal case is very different from what she's actually doing. In the case she's positioned as the possession of her husband. But the content of the evidence suggests that she did not see herself that way at all. How do we then reconcile that contradiction and what can we understand about her? The students find it frustrating that none of the documents is actually from her point of view. So what can we glean about this woman and her experiences? Those kinds of stories can also be helpful—to hand them certain things and say, "Okay, read this. What do you think?"

And then say, "*Why* do you think that?" Students are not used to that question and get perplexed. But it's a good question for getting them to examine their assumptions—exploring what they think they know about the past and then getting rid of the false assumptions. After a while, they get it and start asking that question of themselves.

I'd like to switch from undergraduate teaching and curriculum and talk a little bit about graduate students. What's your approach to graduate education?

My approach is basically that there are many ways into the profession, and we all go our own way because our minds work in different ways. My role as a graduate advisor is to help all students realize their potential with the expectation that they absolutely can reach their goals. I have no doubt that they will and it's just a matter of how we're going to do that. Everybody needs something different, and it's my role as an advisor to figure out what each student needs.

If you could offer grad students any advice about studying history, what would it be?

You've got to love it. The reason why we do this is that we really do love it. Carl Smith, the professor who explained graduate school to me, told me that. He said, "You know, the reason why you do this is because you love it." Of course, there will always be moments when you don't like particular aspects of your job. But you should really love being a historian, and if you keep that at the center of what you do, then I think the profession becomes a little bit easier to negotiate.

Ultimately the meritocracy is not perfect in the profession. You will always see people whose work is great and who don't get the job you think they should or the fellowship or just the recognition for their work, and there are people whose work is not so good who are elevated over others. That's the case in individual circumstances, but generally, if your work is good and you are persistent, it will turn out, because it's the work that matters. We are in a profession that judges the work more than anything else, certainly more than is the case with other professions where you need to be beautiful or you need to be glib or you need to have the right connections.

In fact, there are any number of examples of people who didn't know what graduate school was, who came from places where it was unlikely they were going to end up in graduate school, who had no connections, and who still are doing quite well because the scholarship matters so much. If you love the work and you do the work, then the professional issues will take care of themselves.

For most grad students the job market looms in our future, and occasionally people question why we chose this career path. How do you advise students who want to pursue history in such a difficult job market?

At Duke, there are not a lot of undergraduates who want to go into history because the undergraduates there are very much geared toward professional careers. So I'm not really faced with that question from undergraduates very much.

But I do get these questions from graduate students. That said, most of these students have already decided on this path, and they really want to do it. My job, as I see it, is to help them succeed, not discourage them. Having watched people go through graduate school, it's hard to tell who is going to do well and who is not, in the long run, once they get out of graduate school. People who are the stars in the first years of coursework can flame out later and never really do the work that you thought they might do. Then there are people who struggle through coursework but go on to very productive, high-profile careers. It's really hard to pick who's going to succeed.

The same goes for graduate applications. After looking at them for years, I still can't tell—with certainty—who is going to write amazing scholarship. That's impossible to do, with grades, the GREs, an intellectual statement, and a writing sample. I can tell you whom I like or who sounds interesting, but I can't predict the future from those materials. I can go through and tell you who has the strongest file by objective standards, but that person may not ultimately make a great historian because being a great historian is a mix of things. It's about persistence and the desire to do the work. It's about the creativity that you bring to work. And all of that is not something you can really measure in a standardized application.

Because success in the profession is so individualized, there are different ways to conceive of success. Not everybody is going to be at Yale. Not everybody should be at Yale, because you need to succeed in your own way. People should go with their strengths and their goals; I don't really discourage students from crafting their own careers. There are lots of opportunities for discouragement in our society, and there are lots of people who will tell you how you should be cautious in pursuing your dreams. As graduate advisor, my job is to help you get there, not discourage you from doing it. If students decide not to do it, that should be their decision, not mine.

That's very optimistic. That's very encouraging. I have one final question, and this is perhaps an unfair question, but it's something that I don't usually get to ask.

[*Edwards laughs.*]

Of all your different projects, do you have a favorite? And if so, why?

I don't know. I mean in some ways, all my projects are the same project. As you sort of move forward, you realize that's inevitable. It should be the same project to you—the same set of questions that you keep working through. But that project should always look different to other people. If you do the same project and it looks the same to other people, then that's a problem.

It's about your intellectual growth over time. I think because of that, I really do like the last book, because it was the hardest. It was difficult to research. It was difficult to put together. It was difficult beyond belief to write. It was difficult to explain to people what I was trying to do.

It was really challenging and hard, but I also loved working on it. It was consuming, and exciting to work on, and I enjoyed figuring out how to write it. And I enjoyed all of that even as I hated it at the same time. So I think I'm most proud of that book because it was so hard and because I was able to do it in the way that I really wanted to do it. There are still problems with it. I still go back and think, "Oh, I would change that." I hope, ten years from now, that I'll have the same feeling about it that I have for the first book. That this last book would be better if only I knew what I now know ten years down the road.

But—yes, it was the biggest challenge, so it's the one I like the best right now.

NOTE

1. Eric Foner, *Reconstruction: America's Unfinished Revolution, 1863–1877* (New York: Harper & Row, 1988).

3

A Popular Historian

A Conversation with James M. McPherson

Charity R. Carney

James M. McPherson was born in North Dakota and grew up in Minnesota, where he graduated from Gustavus Adolphus College in 1958. Becoming interested in southern history because the South seemed exotic and mysterious to a Minnesota boy, he decided to do his graduate work under C. Vann Woodward at Johns Hopkins, from which he received his PhD in 1963. From 1962 until his retirement in 2004, he taught at Princeton University, where he is now the George Henry Davis '86 Professor of American History Emeritus. He is the author of more than fifteen books, mostly on the era of the Civil War, and the editor of another ten. His books have won several prizes, most notably the Pulitzer Prize (1989) for *Battle Cry of Freedom: The Civil War Era* (Oxford University Press, 1988) and two Lincoln Prizes (1998 and 2009) for *For Cause and Comrades: Why Men Fought in the Civil War* (Oxford University Press, 1997) and *Tried by War: Abraham Lincoln as Commander in Chief* (Penguin Press, 2008). He is a member of several professional associations and an elected member of the Society of American Historians, the American Philosophical Society, and the American Academy of Arts and Sciences. He has served as president of the Society of American Historians and the American Historical Association.

This interview, conducted in early 2006, opens with McPherson's description of a work in progress (which became *Tried by War*) before moving into a broader discussion of his career.

Please tell us a little bit about what you are currently working on.

Well, what I'm working on now is a book about Abraham Lincoln. But I haven't thought of the actual title yet. It was suggested by a publisher who said that a classic study of Lincoln and his generals was now more than fifty years old and it was a good idea to take another look at the subject. I was a little bit hesitant at first to take on the project, but the more I thought about it, I knew it was something I could do and wanted to do. I have a wider conception of the nature of the topic than is found in T. Harry Williams's book,[1] which is a good book and stands up fairly well, but it focuses almost entirely on Lincoln's relationships with his generals and the way in which he envisioned the military elements of the Civil War. But I think he saw his role as commander in chief in a wider perspective. Such issues as the Emancipation Proclamation became part of his role as commander in chief, and in fact he justified the Emancipation Proclamation on the basis of his war powers as commander in chief to seize any property being used to wage war against the United States. So an issue like emancipation and the whole question of civil liberties, [the suspension of the writ of] habeas corpus, and martial law were all part of his effort to win the war. So I will be writing a book about Lincoln's role as president in wartime and how he tried to achieve the goal of preserving the United States. And his chief preoccupation in that role was the military, but there were other things such as civil liberties, emancipation, and even the mobilization of the polity that were related to the political process to support the war. Such things as appointing Democrats to important offices to unite the North so that it wouldn't just be a Republican war. All of these were part of this effort, and that is how I'm going to do the book.

Sounds like it will be controversial.

I'm sure it will be controversial. Some of these issues I've actually written about in an essay, parts of which will be incorporated in the book, on Lincoln's invention of what we call "war powers." He was the first president to use them and he used them twice. In his first message to the special session of Congress in 1861, he talked about a number of things he had done under war powers between the outbreak of the war in April and the meeting of Congress in July, including the suspension of writ of habeas corpus. Since then, presidential war powers have been used and are highly controversial today, and by implication they are related to what Lincoln did on many occasions that was controversial then, so there is contemporary relevance to some of these issues.

With your current research on Lincoln and the higher echelon and previous research on common soldiers, have those perspectives changed your views on the Civil War?

Well, yes, I suppose they have. In some ways, I was always interested in how this war, more than any other war in US history, could mobilize a whole population for four years and was the principal preoccupation for almost all people in both the Confederacy and the Union. It was a fact that they could not escape. It affected their lives far more in the South, in their own homes, which was not true for people in the North. But I looked at the Civil War from the experience of the soldiers in the ranks and their families, since most of my evidence includes letters to and from their families. You start looking at things from the bottom up and the top down, and rely on both of the perspectives to discover the ways in which the war affected everyone's lives. I think that's probably true for the Civil War more than any other civil experience, with a whole people preoccupied and obsessed, twenty-four hours a day, seven days a week, with this war. Americans at other times—maybe World War II, but World War II was fought thousands of miles away—and most parts of the United States were safe from being directly affected by the war. But that just wasn't true in the Civil War, especially in the South. So it changed their lives and this research helped me understand the ways in which it changed their lives.

Was the all-encompassing nature of the Civil War what first attracted you to study the war?

I wouldn't call it the all-encompassing nature that attracted me to the Civil War, although there were some dimensions of that. When I first went to graduate school at Johns Hopkins in Baltimore, I had a vague notion that I was interested in the history of the South. Of course, I had virtually never been to the South. I grew up in Minnesota. I suppose you could say that Minnesota is about as far away from the South as you can be in the United States, physically and culturally. But I became fascinated by the South because of the beginnings of the civil rights movement and the clashes that were going on in the South. And so there was something kind of exotic and strange about the South that I thought I could learn more about.

I went to college and was interested in American history, but basically twentieth-century history and not the Civil War. But I did develop this interest in the South. So I went to Hopkins and C. Vann Woodward was my advisor there—he was the foremost historian of the South at the time. During my first year at Hopkins I got very much interested in Reconstruction. The reason I got interested in Reconstruction was because Baltimore was a big city and the civil rights movement was affecting Baltimore with protests and sit-ins in restaurants, and by 1960 and 1961 the whole city was affected by sit-ins and the Freedom Riders were on their way through the South. I was surrounded by that, it was my world in the 1960s—my local world of Baltimore and larger world of the United States. I was certainly struck by the parallels between the early 1960s and 1860s, the confrontation between the national government and southern political leaders. George Wallace and Massive Resistance and standing in the schoolhouse door. Federal troops being sent down to the South. On a vastly different scale those things were happening in the 1860s, especially in the Lower South. So that was what attracted me initially to the Civil War. And I chose for my own dissertation something [related]—the role of what I call the civil rights activists of the 1860s and their vision of what should come after emancipation from slavery. So I took that as my dissertation and it became my first book. And that was my entrée into the Civil War.

I wasn't really that interested initially in the military aspects of the Civil War, and my interest in the political aspects was really focused on this specialized issue—the transformation and changing role of the federal government and the role of these civil rights activists. So these are the people

I studied, but as I went on I became more and more convinced that everything they were able to accomplish depended on the role of politics in government and in turn, during the war itself, everything the government was able to do depended on the army. So my interest broadened from my initial interest in these activist performers to the government to the army. I became rather eclectic in my interest in the Civil War over time, though my initial interest was this civil rights activism.

You mentioned C. Vann Woodward. In his work, he makes direct connections between the past and the present. Did that influence you in your work?

It influenced me from almost the very beginning. As an incoming graduate student, I had an appointment before classes started in the fall of 1958 to introduce myself to Woodward. So the interview was set up for such and such a day in September 1958, and when the time came I got a phone call and he changed the date of the interview because he had been called to testify before Congress on the continuing issue of desegregation in Little Rock. This was the second year but it was still contentious. Since he had written a famous book, *The Strange Career of Jim Crow*, and he had written many magazine articles about the question of race relations in the South comparing contemporary issues to the history of these relations, he was an expert witness for this committee.[3] That was an eye-opening experience for me. Here was a historian who wrote mainly about the nineteenth century who was called to testify about a contemporary issue, which demonstrated to me more dramatically than anything else could have done just how relevant history and historians could be to understanding the world in which we live today. So I've always seen history as a way of helping us understand our own contemporary world. Of course, my experience—and being influenced in my choice of a dissertation topic by events that were going on in my contemporary world—was just further proof of the kind of two-way street between the past and the present. And that has been my philosophy of history ever since.

Many people have misunderstandings about what historians do, some labeling them as "revisionist" or "biased," especially when they make connections between the past and the present. How would you defend the academy against such criticism?

I would defend them by saying that the ideal for every historian is to be as objective as possible—to try to understand the past on its own terms, to try to understand all points of view in the past about a contentious issue, to understand why people acted the way they did without comparing it to the present. That is the ideal. But the ideal is not the reality. It is impossible for anybody to completely escape the influence of the present world. It's only common sense to admit that we have cultural predilections based on how we were brought up, whether we are black or white, male or female, live in the North or South, are Anglo or Hispanic, or whatever it's going to be. These are just facts of life. Although we try to escape whatever biases, sometimes subconscious biases, that that creates when we look at the past, we try to shed our contemporary persona and put ourselves back into the past. But it's impossible. History should be what happened in the past, but in the real world history is what historians see in the past. I'm Historian A, but Historians B, C, and D are going to see something differently than I do. And that is what makes history interesting—people have different perspectives. So I will write a book or an article on the significance of the Emancipation Proclamation, but someone else who has a different perspective on that is going to write a book or an article that says something different. And that's good. If we all said the same thing about the Emancipation Proclamation, or anything else that happened in the past like that, history would be pretty dull. Just a recitation of so-called facts. But it really isn't something like that—it's life, and it's dynamic, it's controversial. That's what makes history interesting. And that's what I would tell people who say it's biased. Of course it's biased, but the bias should be kept under control. And the bias—or the perspective I prefer to call it—is what makes it interesting. And it makes history something alive rather than something that's dead. But it's all too often taught that way, as a recitation, especially in high school. But we know that it's not.

What was working with Woodward like? Did you have a good relationship?

I had a good relationship with him, although interestingly enough I got to know him better as a friend after graduate school. I think any graduate student has a kind of deference to a professor. I don't regret not calling him "Vann" when I was a student; in fact it took me a long time afterward to call him by his first name. But I did have a good relationship with him, but not a close friendship the way it eventually became. He was not what I would call a "hands-on" mentor. He allowed students to do what they wanted to do. He was a good critic of what they wrote, but he did not try to dictate the subjects that they chose or the way they approached those subjects. He was kind of laissez-faire about it. He was there when a student needed him or wanted to ask him questions or consult with him about something but did not go out of his way to be on top of his students every week. And I like that kind of relationship. I hear stories about other academic advisors who tell students that they have to do a dissertation on such and such and then are heavy-handed. Woodward was the opposite. So I had a good relationship with him.

Hopkins had really started out as a graduate school based largely on the German model of a professional graduate institution. A lot of American academic historians in the late nineteenth century had gotten their professional training in the German system and brought the model to the United States and that model was strongest at Hopkins. And that legacy still lingered on when I was there. Hopkins was both a graduate and an undergraduate school, but the undergraduate program kind of got short shrift. So in the history program, for example, many of the courses were combined graduate and undergraduate courses. If it was a lecture or quasi-lecture course it would be small, thirty people, basically what was a seminar with half graduate and half undergraduate. The courses I took with Vann and with other professors at Hopkins would be about twenty-five or thirty of us around a famous table that had been there at the time of Frederick Jackson Turner and Woodrow Wilson that Hopkins still used. Everything was geared toward the graduate students. So Woodward was basically speaking to the graduate students. He was not what you call a good lecturer or good teacher in the sense that undergraduates did not really understand much and his lecture style was low-key and dry. He would not have been an effective or attractive teacher for a large undergraduate course, or even a small undergraduate course. But he was very effective with graduate students. That was fine with me, but I always felt sorry for the undergraduates. Things are different at Hopkins now, more traditional, and graduate and undergraduate programs are more separated with a lot more resources than when I was there.

Did you find that you patterned the way that you interact with your students after how you interacted with Woodward?

Well, with graduate students I did. I try to allow them as much scope as possible to develop their own opinion, approach to history, to write about what they want to. Princeton in some ways used to be the opposite of Hopkins. When I first came to Princeton in 1962, it was true in the 1960s and even the 1970s that the main focus in history was undergraduate education. There was a small graduate group attached to it, good but small. It was just the opposite at Hopkins where the undergraduates complained that they were overlooked by the institution. At Princeton the graduates complained that they were overlooked by the institution and had fewer resources. That's still largely true, but there is more focus on graduate students. As far as undergraduates are concerned, I really took as my model somewhat of a crackerjack senior professor at Princeton, a terrific lecturer, with a cult following among undergraduates. I thought, "This is how you should teach undergraduates." I don't think that I ever achieved that kind of cult following that Eric Goldman had, but that became my model for teaching undergraduates. I got that at Princeton and not Hopkins.

What is your teaching philosophy? How do you connect with your students?

I don't think it would be anything as elaborate as a philosophy. I guess I connect with students in an effort to understand what they are interested in. It creates feedback. The first time I would teach any course, I would try to be sensitive to any feedback I got. I'm talking now, I guess, mainly about undergraduates. What's working and what's not working and try to adjust to students' feedback. If that's a philosophy, then that's mine. I mean, I'm the expert on the subject so the content of the subject is something that provides a basic framework, but the techniques of getting that information across or the types of questions about that information students might have that are not made clear in my lecture I try to explain to them. You get feedback from students—they like this book you assigned, they don't like that book, they like the way you did something, they don't like the way you did something else. That's important and I think a professor should adjust to that. In other words, the course isn't taught the way students think it ought to be taught, but what they think about is important and so is the professor arriving at the way it can be most effective. So it's a two-way kind of relationship, it should be a two-way kind of relationship. There's an audience and a speaker, but the audience is a participant in the process and ought to be kept in mind. If that's a philosophy, that's mine.

You started taking classes on battlefield tours. How did that come about?

It was actually suggested initially by a graduate student named Walter Licht who had taken a couple of grad seminars with me and was a teaching assistant in my undergraduate course on the Civil War and Reconstruction.

He said, "Why don't we take the students who want to go on a big trip to Gettysburg?" I said, "OK." The first time we did it, people didn't take it. Then I didn't do it for a couple of years. Someone else suggested it, and I gave a little more publicity to it, and it just grew from there. By the time I did my last one two years ago, I had to separate the group [into two parts] [*laughs*]. There were lots of townspeople and parents. The last time I taught the course, two years ago, I had the son of a senator in my class and his niece—they were both in the class. They went on the trip and told him about it, and he turned up and wanted to go. I would always have lots of parents and townspeople. The president [of Princeton] in recent years has made big lecture courses open to people who want to come and sit in. And I would always take them. So it became a kind of community event. Always to Gettysburg, which is the closest and one that people are interested in.

That brings me to a question about both your academic and nonacademic audiences. Your most famous work, the Pulitzer Prize-winning* Battle Cry of Freedom*, has been read by an extremely broad audience. How did you navigate writing for both general and academic readers?

Well, I've often thought about that, and I don't have a conscious technique for doing that. I just try to write in such a way that an intelligent, interested reader, whether a student, an academic peer, or just a member of the general public, can find it interesting and worthwhile and educational. I don't sit down and say, "I'm going to write it this way because. . . ." It just happens that way. Maybe it's a consequence of life experiences. But Woodward did the same thing. If you take a look at *The Strange Career of Jim Crow* or some of his essays in *The Burden of Southern History* or some of his other books, they appealed to a very wide audience, not just an audience of specialists.[2] So I might have picked it up from him through osmosis if nothing else. And to go back to that experience that I mentioned a few minutes ago, my appointment being changed because he had to go testify before Congress, here's a historian who is speaking to a broader public audience because he has something to say of importance and interest to them, and in this case it's very specialized. But clearly he is speaking to a broader audience. It may just be from day one that that became my model for what a historian could do or should try to do—speak to multiple audiences. Speaking in his own voice but also in a voice that can be understood by a layperson. I strongly believe that historians do have a responsibility to speak to an audience beyond specialists. I think that every historian has to serve an apprenticeship, with a dissertation or a couple of journal articles. That's the apprenticeship you serve learning your craft, and that's likely not to appeal to the broad audience out there. But over time, as the historian gains knowledge and gains some perspective on things, I think the historian does have the responsibility to try to bring his or her knowledge to a broad public audience. Because the public audience, whether it be members of Congress or anyone, are all citizens and all need to know about the world around them and society, and they are not going to know much about these issues if they don't know the historical context. So historians have something important to say. Political leaders, presidents, members of Congress, who don't know the historical background about these things, are likely to not be able to intelligently make decisions. Even Karl Rove had President Bush reading American history. I wish he had read a little bit more, earlier [*laughs*].

Do you think that the profession has contributed to or detracted from the merit of writing narrative history—history that would be considered "popular"? Do you think the profession's opinion of popular history has changed at all in recent years?

It certainly has changed in lip service. Starting in the 1980s but especially in the 1990s there were a number of articles and a couple of presidential addresses at the American Historical Association [AHA] about the need for historians to speak to a broader audience and to do so in the format of narrative history. My colleague at Princeton, Lawrence Stone, in his AHA presidential address talked about this whole issue of returning to narrative history in the 1990s. So there was a lot of concern among historians that the profession would become increasingly developed, so incestuous that they spoke only to each other and wrote specialized articles and specialized books with certain jargon that no one else could understand. There was a lot of lip service given to the idea of writing to a broader audience. The series in which *Battle Cry* appeared was conceived of and edited by Richard Hofstadter and was premised on the idea that these books would be the latest in professional scholarship directed to a broad audience in narrative format. So that idea has been out there for quite a while now. And I think it has had some kind of impact, but there is a countervailing pressure within the profession, and that is that if your books appeal to too many people then you are a "popularizer." And "popularizer" is a bad word because it seems to imply a lack of serious scholarship, the lack of any kind of breakthrough search or methodological techniques. You are not advancing knowledge, you are retailing it to the masses. So especially for younger historians there is a feeling that if they write something that a junior in high school would find interesting, it's no good. Therefore, they write to other academic peers or graduate students or professors, and they can show they can use words like "paradigm" or some of the other jargon. And in a way I suppose that's OK, that's part of the apprenticeship. But I think that for those who are capable of doing it, they should begin to write for a broader audience. Maybe after they get tenure or something, because to get tenure you show your colleagues that you are right up there with the "cutting edge." All of these clichés—"cutting edge" is good, "popularizing" is bad. These have become clichés or stereotypes that we should get away from, but they still exist.

Do you think there are stereotypes related to writing or teaching military history today?

Yes, I think there are. Although that I believe has changed some in the last ten years or so, partly because our definition of military history, or some people's definition of military history, has broadened. There is still the stereotype that military history, and not just about the Civil War, consists of studying battles and campaigns and that kind of thing. It certainly does consist of that; it is at the core of it. But in the last fifteen or twenty years our understanding of military history has broadened out. It has been influenced much by social history. Who are the people who constitute armies, what kind of social backgrounds do they come from, what do they bring into the army in the way of political assumptions, religious convictions, and so on? All of this is part of military history, as it is now much more broadly defined. How does it relate to society, to culture, how does it relate to the trinity of gender, race, and class? I think that there is lots of good military history being written of this sort that has gained a good deal more academic respectability. But there are still two separate worlds, and sometimes the communication between them that should exist does not, and they are kept separate. One trumpets the old-fashioned military history, and then there is this other kind of broader military history that we are talking about. But the broader military history often does not have as much popular appeal. Some of the books that do best in military history tend to be of the old-fashioned kind. But even the old-fashioned variety has broadened. Some of the really good campaign studies and narratives now do bring in some of these techniques of this broader concept of military history. They emphasize more what the people in the ranks are experiencing. So the old-fashioned are still worth reading, but they have very little at the center. These kinds of things are still very popular, but military history in the broader sense has gained some academic respectability. There are still stereotypes associated with doing military history. But there are a number of institutions with strong academic programs in military history or individuals who teach at these institutions who are really good. One at Ohio State and institutions like Virginia, North Carolina, and so on. A lot of others as well do good things. I think they have raised the reputation of military history above the old stereotype. They are trying to be—another word I don't like—a "crossover" from an academic to a broad general audience. When I first heard myself described as a "crossover historian," I thought, "I don't like the sound of that." But now it's become acceptable, and I understand it.

Considering what we discussed before concerning the connection between the past and the present, do you think the trend to incorporate social and cultural history in military history is positive?

I do. A very positive thing. There was a kind of delay, and this happened more than there needed to be because social history has been the most dynamic, broadly defined, kind of development within the academic, historical profession for the last thirty years, I suppose, since the 1960s. But as it was forging ahead in the 1960s, 1970s, and 1980s, there was a kind of reaction against military history primarily because of opposition to American policy in Vietnam, which was especially strong within the academic community. So military history had a really bad reputation just because it somehow seemed to be connected to Vietnam. And I think it's only as we've been removed from the Vietnam era since the 1980s that this kind of delayed effort to incorporate social history dynamically into military history really moved ahead. So it's been a development over the past twenty years. It's still relatively new, and it took some time for something new like that to overcome all these stages.

What advice would you give graduate students who would like to study the Civil War? How can they find new perspectives or new insight in such a crowded field?

One way to do it, and it's been the way it's been done by many, is localized or specialized studies—a certain community during the war or particular groups during the war. There have been a lot of good regional community studies of the war, mostly of southern communities, because there are a lot more details during the Civil War of that central area in Virginia or North Carolina or whatever it might be than studying Detroit, Michigan, or Portland, Maine. The Civil War did have an impact there, of course, but not the same kind of thing. So a lot of these studies are of southern communities. And also studies of women during the Civil War. Every one of these soldiers had mothers, wives, sisters, and, of course, the home-front communities mobilized with hospitals and relief societies and the US Sanitary Commission and all of these other kinds of organizations. So studies like that, but sometimes these studies become overdone. After you study ten communities in Virginia, you could study eleven or twelve at that point. One fascinating development that there are a couple of books on is children's literature, on all kinds of books for kids that were published during and after the war. So there are some niches for studies there, and in some ways they might become almost as redundant as the kind of community studies in social history. There are a lot of people who do these kinds of studies, but they all add up to a unique view of the Civil War. Some of that work is going on and needs to go on.

To allude to a subject that we are both interested in, religion, for a long time there were few books about religion in the Civil War. But we are becoming more and more aware that in the nineteenth century, especially in the middle of the nineteenth century, religion was central to people's lives much more so than it is today and more so than previously recognized. Yet for a long time there wasn't much about religion in the Civil War—this cultural context in which people functioned and viewed the world. But now we are more focused on that and it is an important area for further investigation. So I think that even though it's a crowded field, it's such a rich field, and the evidence is so rich with a large number of people being affected. I mean, all those numbers of books and sermons being published during the Civil War—they are just abundant. With these rich resources, there really are plenty.

What were some of the challenges you faced in writing your dissertation?

One challenge I faced was skepticism on the part of some of my peers and scholars at other institutions about whether they agreed that there was something important there. It was a fairly widespread assumption at the time that once slavery was abolished, the mission of the abolitionists ended. Many of them had devoted decades of their lives to this crusade against slavery, but once the crusade was over and they actually won, it ended. There really was an assumption in the literature that was reflective of this idea—

that these people went back into the world and lost their sense of distinctiveness and purpose. And I wondered if that was true. I had read enough to think that it was perhaps not true. In some ways just getting peer approval or professional approval for this topic as a viable one was the most important obstacle that I faced. As I started doing research, I became convinced that there was a lot there, but it took a while to overcome that skepticism. It wasn't until after I wrote it up that I was able to convince people there was something to the book. I suppose that there are a lot of graduate students who are writing their dissertations who may face the same kind of thing. And some students do decide after they start on a particular project that either there isn't enough there or they are not as interested as they thought they would be. That's the real danger with having your academic advisor point you in a direction with the dissertation. It's not your choice, it's somebody else's choice, but you are going to have to spend a lot of time on it. And unless you are really absorbed with the project, it's difficult to spend the time and effort doing the research. Unless you continue to be absorbed by the subject it can be problematic. So the choice of the dissertation topic ought to be yours and not someone else's.

Can you describe the process of taking the dissertation through publication into a book? Was it difficult for you to get the dissertation published?

It turned out not to be very difficult. When I finished the dissertation I was in my first year teaching at Princeton. Princeton University Press had some kind of a mechanism for all new young faculty who came to Princeton. Somebody from the press contacted them early on and said, "Well, you know once you have your dissertation done, would it be something that we might be interested in?" And I had thought about publication, but I had never thought much about what I would do to start that ball rolling. But they contacted me before I had finished a draft of the dissertation. In the first year there, I was producing with Woodward, and I worked two years on the dissertation. I was getting it prepared. So it wasn't done yet, and I told the people at Princeton University Press, "Here is my dissertation topic." This was of course in 1963 at a time when there was enormous public interest in the civil rights movement, you know, what was going on right here in Alabama, especially in Birmingham. That created a national implication for civil rights, and of course much of the rhetoric of the civil rights movement in particular emphasized the same kinds of things that the abolitionists had one hundred years earlier. In fact, activists tried to get President Kennedy to issue a new kind of Emancipation Proclamation. Originally Kennedy was still controlled by Congress, the congressional majority, and his own party was in control in Washington. And so not much came of it. There was the contemporary interest, which is what got me interested in the subject in the first place and created a broad general interest. So the people at Princeton University Press said they would be interested. Once it was done I sent them the dissertation and they offered me a contract. I didn't even have to revise it that much. So it was pretty easy.

*Would you say things have changed a bit since then? [*Laughs.*]*

Well, a lot of things have changed since then. It was easy to get a job in those days, too.

How did you go about getting the job at Princeton?

The chairman of the department at Princeton called up Vann Woodward one day and said, "Do you have any young men?"

Really?

There were hardly any women historians. Some. Princeton, of course, was a male institution. There were women, but they were pretty rare. This is 1962. So he said, "Do you have any young men? We're hiring instructors in history." In those days that was a tenure-track appointment. And he said, "I have someone in mind." So I went to New York City to the AHA and interviewed with four or five senior professors. And we just chatted for a while. It was not formal. And they offered me the job. I had to do nothing.

They offered you a job on the spot?

Almost on the spot. I think a letter came from the institution. The truth is that I was born of the right gender and race at the right time in American history. I was born in 1936, during the depth of the Depression. So I was a part of a birth cohort that was one of the smallest in the twentieth century. And I was coming of age and on the job market when the first of the children of the postwar baby boom were about to enter college. So there were few people in my birth cohort and suddenly they needed people to teach all of these new students. Jobs came looking for us; we didn't have to go looking for jobs. There were more jobs than there were candidates for jobs. Most of my classmates and contemporaries at Hopkins didn't have to go looking for a job. They may have applied to one or two places, but the application process was different. Here's my field and interests, my credentials, and eventually they got the job. All of my classmates got jobs at pretty good institutions. Princeton, of course, is one of the best, but there were others who got good jobs. In those days, white males were the norm. It was much harder for women to get a job. We were several years away from it being an advantage. It all changed later, but it changed at a time when it became much harder for everybody to get a job. So I can empathize and understand the difficulties that people face today in getting a job. But I didn't have to go through that experience myself. I suppose I ought to feel a bit guilty.

What advice would you give graduate students who are going to be entering the job market, realizing that you did not have to go through the same process yourself but based on what you have seen?

Well, the advice I give is pretty standard. You need to apply to multiple jobs and consider carefully the cover letter you send. When you go to an interview there are things that you need to do to be prepared, brush your hair and dress well [*laughs*]. I don't have any secrets. I suppose the most important advice is to be yourself. Present yourself well. And be prepared to be disappointed. As a faculty member and mentor of students it's difficult to see students apply for a job and really want to get it, and especially if they are one of the top three and it does not come through. It can be just really devastating. I tell them, "It's not a reflection of you, it's a reflection of the situation. There are more people looking for jobs, some of them who are looking for jobs or already had jobs that are only temporary that you are competing with." So it is hard.

It sounds like there was a network set up when you were going through the process.

The old boy network [*laughs*].

I wasn't going to call it that. . . .

That's exactly what it was.

Do you think it still exists in some form or fashion or has it been overturned?

I think that it's largely been overturned, at least based on my experiences as a faculty member. Certainly in the institutional framework, so everybody starts equally when applying for a job. At least in my experience, search committees carefully read through without necessarily privileging a PhD from Harvard, etcetera. However, if a professor from Harvard who is pretty famous writes a letter to a search committee, that letter of recommendation still carries weight. That's not necessarily the old boy network—it is more of a boy or a girl network—but there still is something. But I would say it's mostly disappeared.

It's not positive for people looking for jobs, but do you think it's good for the profession to have so many people in it?

It has really been important for smaller colleges, what we call second- or third-tier institutions. They are getting much better faculty. It is so competitive that really good people who want to teach are willing to take a job at an institution that has less prestige because it is a job. So really good people are teaching at institutions where forty years ago they did not have them. It's good for undergraduates at these second-tier institutions. There's a bit of a downside to it because sometimes people who are really good and their reputation is that they do a really good job wind up not happy and thinking about trying to get out. So there's a downside to it. They are good people but think they are too good for where they are. The situation is improving. My sense of it is that [the situation] is improving, but it will not be like it was for me.

It doesn't sound like it ever will be.

No, I don't think it ever will be. And now there's an institutional framework where every job is open. You can't just call up one or two people and say, "Do you want this job? We are keeping it a secret." You can't do that anymore.

Do you think graduate programs and graduate students have changed a lot since you were in school?

There is much more diversity. The work of graduate students has changed, with the development of social and cultural history studies. It's much richer and more cosmopolitan, which is good. And I think that also the number of what I call "specialization" histories have increased, such as social history and cultural history and so on. There were only a few students who studied things like East Asian history or South Asian history when I was in school. Now I think that East Asian history and South Asian history are burgeoning fields. It's much richer.

Do you think that the diversity of students has influenced the diversity of the fields?

Yes, I think so.

Is there anything about the current state of the profession or graduate school that you believe should change?

Most graduate programs are subconsciously dedicated to—or most graduate advisors are subconsciously devoted to—creating clones of themselves: "The ideal career is my career." In other words, to teach at a university and do research, that's the role model. And so if a student decides not to teach at a university, he rejects that model. Suppose you get a job as a historical advisor for the park service. You feel and probably your graduate advisor feels that you are a great disappointment, you are a failure. In other words, I think that students ought to be aware and professors ought to get over the mindset that the top of the professional ladder is the professor at a research institution. Things like teaching at a small liberal arts college, going into the National Park Service as a historian, doing public history, or being a museum director is what we need historians to do. These are jobs where you can have just as much impact. But that is not what we have and that is too bad.

Is that a similar sort of mentality as disliking "popularizing" history?

I think so; that is probably the same thing going on. It's an insular world. I think that it needs to try in both respects. But there are powerful countervailing forces. I think we need to be aware of it. I think that the profession is more aware of it. There is lip service given to appealing to a broader audience, but we need more than lip service.

Do you think that history would be more important if we actually reached out more?

Yes, I do. Huge numbers of people visit venues where they learn history. A lot more people than take a university course go to historical sites or watch the History Channel, A&E, PBS. So there are lots of venues where people learn history. The better that is done, the better our citizens will become. One of George Rable's graduate colleagues ended up working at the park in Petersburg. [Will Greene is the executive director of Pamplin Park and the Museum of the Civil War Soldier in Petersburg.] That's the route he chose to go, and he's done a great job. Tens of thousands of people—probably more people visit that museum than attend Rable's classes [*laughs*]. So you can contribute in that way.

Even if a student is interested in entering the profession in a more traditional way, you would recommend that they do something with public history.

Yes. A lot of times we can use our knowledge and experience to bring information to a broad audience. It's challenging but well worth it. We all learn from other people. Any question—even a stupid one—is worth asking if you learn something from it.

What has kept you in the profession for so long? How have you remained so productive?

I enjoy it. I would do it all over again. As far as being productive, teaching at a university like Princeton, it's still an institution that encourages productivity. If I had taught at an institution that was not as supportive, it might not have been the same. I was just basically lucky to be in that kind of setting. It encouraged me to work very hard.

NOTES

1. T. Harry Williams, *Lincoln and His Generals* (New York: Alfred A. Knopf, 1952).
2. C. Vann Woodward, *The Strange Career of Jim Crow* (New York: Oxford University Press, 1955).
3. C. Vann Woodward, *The Burden of Southern History* (Baton Rouge: Louisiana State University Press, 1960).

4

No Better Way to Spend Your Life

A Conversation with Gary W. Gallagher

Glenn David Brasher

Gary W. Gallagher currently holds the prestigious title of John L. Nau III Professor in the History of the American Civil War at the University of Virginia. Before joining the faculty at Virginia in 1998, he was a professor at Pennsylvania State University, where he also served as head of their history department. A native of Los Angeles, California, he received his BA from Adams State College of Colorado (1972) and his MA (1977) and PhD (1982) from the University of Texas at Austin. He is the author or editor of more than thirty books, including *The Confederate War* (Harvard

University Press, 1997), *Lee and His Generals in War and Memory* (Louisiana State University Press, 1998), *Causes Won, Lost, and Forgotten: How Hollywood and Popular Art Shape What We Know about the Civil War* (University of North Carolina Press, 2008), and *The Union War* (Harvard University Press, 2011). He serves as editor of Civil War America, a series at the University of North Carolina Press with more than one hundred titles to date, and has appeared in more than three dozen television projects on the subject.

In this conversation, conducted in Charlottesville in 2004, Gallagher speaks candidly of his college experiences, his opinions of the graduate school process, and his thoughts on the history profession. Along the way he shares interesting insights on teaching, American race relations, and why historians should reach out to popular audiences. He then concludes with strong advice for all graduate students working in history.

Tell us about your undergraduate career at Adams State College.

I grew up on a farm in southern Colorado, and I went to a small liberal arts college close by, Adams State College. I found myself in a wonderful situation for somebody interested in history. The department was headed by Norma Lois Peterson, who was a rigorous scholar, and she had collected this great group of historians who all had their doctorates. The school only had about 2,500 students, but the history department was this powerhouse within that context. They lavished attention on students who were really interested in history, and I got to spend an enormous amount of time talking to professors.

Given your experiences, do you think that it is preferable to go to a small college as an undergraduate rather than to a large university?

I think you can get a wonderful undergraduate education at a large university. Here at Virginia we have great people on the history faculty. Everybody teaches big undergraduate classes. I teach hundreds of students every year, but do they have easy access to me? They really don't. I do some things to try to give more access. I always hold my office hours, but if you have 150 students in a class and you have three office hours in a week, that is not easy for the student. I don't pretend to learn people's names in a class. But in every class I took at Adams State, everybody knew who I was, and I could go by my instructors' offices on a regular basis. You cannot get that here. The only students who do are the really proactive ones who will come to my office hours and talk about things. I am happy to talk to them, but if there are ten students waiting to see me, I can't sit down and talk to them for an hour. So I think there is a huge advantage to being in a small program at a really good, small liberal arts school where you pay $40,000 to have access to people. It's hard to do here. We have an honors college here—most schools do—where you get more access. But for the typical student, it's much easier to just float along the stream.

It's just not the same as at a smaller college. I had two of my graduate professors at Texas comment about the fact that in my first semester as a graduate student I arrived with a better grasp of American historiography than any other undergraduate they had seen. And the reason was that I had had this wonderful access to my professors at Adams State. I wasn't smarter than any of the other students, but I had had a different experience. That experience is wonderful. It's hard to replicate at a big school.

You started graduate school at Texas in 1973. Why did you apply there?

Because of my professor, John E. McDaniel. When I interviewed at Texas the first time, the outgoing graduate advisor told me: "We can't keep you out of here because of your GREs and your undergraduate work, but you can't come from a school like Adams State College and make it in a serious program." So that was very cheerful news. As I was leaving his office, by sheer serendipity I bumped into Lewis L. Gould, who is an eminent Gilded Age/Progressive Era historian. He was the incoming graduate officer, and for some reason he asked me who I was. I answered and told him about John McDaniel, one of my professors at Adams State, who had been a student of Gould's at Texas. Gould said, "Let me see your stuff." He's a very efficient kind of guy, and he sort of thumbed through my records and said, "What did the other person tell you?" I said that he had told me not to come, that I wouldn't make it. "Oh," Gould said, "batting .360 even in Triple A is a pretty good sign you might do well. You should come, you will do fine."

Whom did you study with at Texas?

I studied with mainly three people at Texas, and the most important one was my major professor, Barnes Fletcher Lathrop, who had been a student of Charles W. Ramsdell. Ramsdell was a great figure at Texas for a long time in southern and Confederate history, and Lathrop took his place. Lathrop never published his dissertation. He wrote a study of sugar planters in Louisiana during the Civil War. Louisiana State University Press offered him a contract, but Lathrop was an unbelievable perfectionist and never could turn loose of it. It was 1,200 pages long at the time of his death. The only book he published was a little book on migration into East Texas. He was an officer in the Southern Historical Association, an original member, and he and his wife had done a pioneer microfilming project in the 1930s—the Ramsdell Microfilm Collection. It's film of hundreds of thousands of documents concerning southern history from all over the country.

I was his last PhD. He had forty-five or fifty.

What did you like best about graduate school?

I loved engagement with the mid-nineteenth century. The Civil War had always been my love, but everyone told me that I needed to do something other than the Civil War, and certainly something other than military history, which was right. This was about 1974, and that is when the new political history was really new. People like Michael F. Holt and others were doing their first number-crunching studies. Gould wanted me to do my dissertation on the presidential election of 1852 and the demise of the Whig Party. So I said I would do it. I had a string of graduate fellowships at Texas, and they wanted me to pick a title they thought would get a lot of attention.

It was a complete mismatch for me. I am not at all inclined toward political history of that sort, but I pretended to be writing that dissertation for three years. I traveled all over the country doing research, but I didn't write anything. I knew nothing was ever going to come of it, so I finally took an editing job at the LBJ library in the summer of 1976. They hired me to edit a backlog of 125 oral histories. Then they offered me a job as an archivist in 1977. I pretended for about three more years to be working on my dissertation (I had passed my comprehensive exams in 1975), and then I withdrew from the program, which embarrassed the department. I think Lathrop was genuinely upset because they had forced the topic on me. I never tell students what to work on, ever. I might make some general suggestions, but I absolutely don't believe in assigning topics to people because it's hard enough to write a dissertation about something you are really interested in. It's impossible to write a dissertation on something you are not really interested in. But the point is Lathrop was upset. He said, "What if we let you do a dissertation on something you are interested in? We can give you fifteen months." I said, "I can't research and write a dissertation in fifteen months." But he said that I would have a big head start in lots of ways and to see if I could find something.

A friend of mine who was in the program, Allan Purcell, ran across a reference to this great collection of papers at the Southern Historical Collection in Chapel Hill—the Steven Dodson Ramseur Papers, which nobody had ever really used. It comprised several hundred letters, which made Ramseur a good potential topic. I went to Chapel Hill and checked the papers out to see what they were really like. There were two sets of letters: a set to the woman he married and a set to his best friend, David Schenck, who became a Superior Court judge in North Carolina after the war—a great set of public issue letters and a great set of very private, revealing letters. Ramseur was mortally wounded at the battle of Cedar Creek, so it's not a long life I was dealing with—he was only twenty-seven when he died. So there's great West Point material and really good Civil War material, and Ramseur was important enough to merit looking at. And so I thought I would use Ramseur as a typical figure of the junior rising command of the Army of Northern Virginia.

Lathrop said go ahead. I have always thought that the reason the Department of History came back to me was that my leaving would have been something of an embarrassment to them. It would have looked bad for the department to have somebody who had a string of fellowships not finish. I thought that's why they pulled me back in.

When you were a graduate student, did you work as a teaching assistant?

I did for just two semesters because I got those fellowships. Well, they called us TAs, but we were really graders; we didn't teach. They didn't have sections in big classes at Texas where they broke them down and actually allowed the TAs to teach. We had mammoth survey classes, 550 to 600 students, and they put three of us in each one, and each would grade between 175 and 200 students.

Did you find it beneficial?

To grade? I found it beneficial listening to the lectures. I TAed for Lew Gould and for George B. Forgie, who were both fabulous lecturers. I learned about teaching big classes, and I learned about the drudgery and utter loathsomeness of grading. It's the worst part of our job.

Tell us about your first academic job.

I was an archivist at the LBJ library while I was finishing my dissertation, and I stayed there for nine years. The year my son graduated from high school, I went on the job market and attended my first American Historical Association [AHA] Conference. I didn't get good mentoring as a graduate student about the profession. There wasn't a sense in the culture of the department at Texas that the faculty should bring you along and show you what it is to be a historian. I didn't get a lot of help in writing my first book reviews, for example, or going to conventions. I take my graduate students now. I introduce them to the culture of the book exhibits, I have them meet some of the editors, and I introduce them to some of the people in the field so they can get a sense of how the conventions work and where the real work is done. I had none of that. So I went to my first AHA because I had interviews, and it was horrifying to me. I am still distinctly uncomfortable at the AHAs. It is a very depressing place to me.

The job market was stressful. There were no jobs in the mid-1970s. Of my cohort at Texas, I think I am the only Americanist who became a practicing historian, and we had a big group of graduate students there. The job market was just unbelievably dismal, and it created a very dark culture among graduate students because there was this sense that no one could get a job. But there were some jobs in 1985–86, and I applied. Out of this process, I had two interviews, one at the University of Cincinnati and one at Penn State. I ended up going to Penn State to replace a man named Warren W. Hassler, who had taught the Civil War there for thirty years.

What kind of survey-level classes did you teach there?

I taught the first half of the US survey. But a major component of that job was to teach courses on naval history and on US military history. They were heavily ROTC in their composition. From the beginning I also taught a Civil War course, so that was my undergraduate rotation. Then my fourth course would be some kind of graduate seminar or undergraduate seminar. I taught the survey for only four years. I gave up the naval history course by the time I became head of the department in 1991.

Comparing Penn State and the University of Virginia, do you notice more or less of a Lost Cause mentality that the students bring with them to their understanding of the Civil War?

There's a little bit more of that at Virginia. There are a lot of people here who have family ties to the Confederacy. That would have been very unusual at Penn State. At Penn State there are many descendants of immigrants whose families came to the United States in the late nineteenth or early twentieth century. However, I don't find a lot of "unreconstructed rebels" here, although there are some. In class when I talk about slavery, they will say, "It's not about slavery; it is about states' rights." I will ask them to list the states' rights that people were asking for, and that really stumps them. They will often say, "My uncle says" or "My father says," and I didn't get that at Penn State, although there were lots of people who loved Robert E. Lee at Penn State. The Lost Cause has pervaded the national understanding of the conflict in a way that the other interpretations of the war that came out of the late nineteenth century really haven't.

It seems it is something that historians have to address by telling the students that they may have to rethink a lot of the things that they were taught about the causes of the Civil War while growing up.

I do a lot of that here, and many students resist—and resist successfully, alas. They come up at the end of the semester and say, "I really enjoyed your class, but I still think you're wrong." Others, however, will say it's been a real revelation. It has to be an act of will to emerge from the other end of the course without ideas challenged someway. It happens, but a lot of students say that they had just never been exposed to this, which I find distressing. I think a lot of high schools and universities don't teach the Civil War at all. They choose not to deal with it. They can deal with Reconstruction more readily because there the villains are pretty clear-cut now, at least in the way that it is presented.

The Civil War is just messy, slavery is messy, and racism is messy, and that is our great bugaboo as a nation. We are still grappling with race every day. It's shot through our culture, whether it's sports or politics or anything, race is there, and it's more complex now because it is a much more complicated mix. We haven't figured race out. We are way ahead of where we were forty years ago, but I think it's just easier for some teachers not to deal with it.

Thavolia Glymph [Associate Professor of African and African American Studies at Duke University] and I were the historical consultants for exhibits at the National Park Service headquarters at Tredegar Iron Works in Richmond. Part of what we did was work with the public, and we also went to meetings of black leaders and "old money" Confederate types in Richmond. I was struck by the degree to which black people just really don't want to get into the Civil War. Reconstruction is seen as the moment when the great promise comes and anticipates the second reconstruction. But to me that is missing the essential first step; you can't even get Reconstruction unless you have the emancipation that comes out of the war. I believe that should be a powerfully attractive subject. The Civil War is the great crucible that does away with slavery. But I think that African Americans are put off by the Civil War, especially in a place like Richmond where the Lost Cause was for decades so pervasive, because they are surrounded by things like Monument Avenue or have everything around them named after Lee or Jackson. There is a Lee-Jackson Day here. Some states even combine MLK and Confederate heroes day; it's bizarre. I think a lot of black people just have their belly full of the Lost Cause so they look somewhere else. They look to Reconstruction.

It's very frustrating. As pivotal an event as the Civil War was to American history, it's even more pivotal, as you say, to African American history. I think that the impression is that emancipation was sort of something that was given to African Americans, and so it is almost seen as being weak because they didn't participate in it that much.

That's another thing for us to argue about. Is it self-emancipation? It's not Lincoln the great emancipator. It's not black people winning their own freedom. It is neither one. People resist complexity. There's not a soundbite answer. You take the United States Army out of that equation and nobody gets freed. I don't care how much you wanted to be free as a slave on the south side of Virginia, if the United States Army doesn't get close enough to make it possible for you to make your way there, or actually come through your town, you're not going to be free.

But you do have to choose to make the US Army an instrument for your freedom.

Of course you do; I'm not saying there isn't "agency," to use a word I have had just about enough of lately. A lot of history now is just a relentless search for agency. Of course there is agency everywhere, but it's also easy, because it makes us feel good, to find more agency than actually is present. Whether we like it or not, powerful white guys were usually in control in American history.

I think what you just said touches on some of the reason there is little interest in Civil War history, because it doesn't seem like an African American story—it's powerful white guys.

It is powerful white guys to a significant extent; if we pretend otherwise we are not dealing honestly with the period. Black people have roles, poor white people have roles, but to try to tell the story without having a significant piece of your emphasis on powerful white guys is going to leave you with a huge part of the story not there. Whether we like it or not we have to take the past as the past was. We can illuminate parts of the past that are useful to us now, but if you are really going to deal honestly with the past you don't do anyone a favor by pretending that something was going on that wasn't. Everybody wants a usable past; that's what a lot of any examination of history is.

I'd like to come back to that later, but for now can you describe the process of getting your first book published?

Well, I think my career shows how capricious this whole world is. There were three finalists for the Penn State job; I was their third choice. My topic was a little too military for many people in the department. In addition, it was Confederate, which was not a plus either, but I got the job because their first choice turned it down, and they decided not to go with their second choice. So I was fortunate there. But the thing is, once you get someplace, you do have agency. If you teach well and publish and so forth, then you are probably going to get ahead.

Chapel Hill published my first book in 1985 just before I went to Penn State. I had sent it to the University of Tennessee Press initially because one of my professors at Texas had a tie to someone there, which is the way things like this work. I saved the two readers' reports because I think they are instructive. They said, "This is a good manuscript. . . . It will be published somewhere, but we don't think the University of Tennessee Press will publish it." They turned it down.

That was the best thing that ever happened to me because within a few months one of the editors from the University of North Carolina Press came through Austin to talk to prospective authors. She and I chatted. Ramseur was a North Carolinian, and Chapel Hill had not published any Civil War books in many years because after the centennial the feeling was that the Civil War was dead. Nobody wanted Civil War books for a long time. But they sent Ramseur out and got recommendations to publish it with some revisions. They published it in 1985, and it did well. It got picked up by the History Book Club and sold several thousand copies, but it never would have gone to Chapel Hill if Tennessee hadn't turned it down.

So I was third in line at Penn State but ended up with a very good job I really liked. And I ended up with this link to Chapel Hill only because the manuscript had been turned down somewhere else. I have had this tremendously productive and wonderful relationship with Chapel Hill for twenty years. I became good friends with Matthew Hodgson, the longtime director of the University of North Carolina Press. He decided the Civil War was something they should publish about again, and I helped find manuscripts—not all military, but some military titles that sold very well. Once I had enough status at Penn State, Matt decided to create the Civil War America series.

Tell us about your experience directing dissertations. What's your philosophy?

My philosophy is to follow the Lathrop model. I don't smother graduate students, although I think I give them a lot of attention at the points where they need it, whether it is taking them to conferences and introducing them around or spending a good deal of time going over drafts of their writing. I use my chair funds here to run a little speaker series just for the graduate students in Civil War. We will have ten or twelve students and first-rank Civil War historians here talking about their projects, how they came to them, the pitfalls, what they are trying to do with them.

So doing those kinds of things for my graduate students is important. I read chapters very carefully. I think I am a good editor, and it's almost impossible for me to read something and not try to improve it. I really think it's important to write clearly, and I don't think we emphasize that nearly enough. In fact I think we reward obtuse writing in our field more and more.

Why do you think that is?

I think many students believe if something is written so clumsily and in such jargon-filled language that they can't really understand it, the author must really be smart, which is pure baloney. The notion that you would write a book for your six friends who work in the field you work in and in inaccessible vocabulary that sets you apart from smart lay readers is ridiculous. It fuels this chasm between the academy and the very large, smart lay readership. If we don't want people to think the Civil War was about states' rights, then write about slavery as a factor in the Civil War in a way that people not only can understand but will also want to read. I think we have abdicated that element of our lives as academics. Some people believe that our role is to advance understanding and never mind what audience we reach. The attitude is that we are a guild, and we are just working for ourselves. I don't believe that, and in the Civil War field I think there is almost an obligation to write for a broader audience, because reaching the audience shouldn't be left in the hands of amateur historians, although there are some very good amateurs in our field.

Is that why you have done so much work for television, like the History Channel?

Yes. I think if you don't do it somebody else will, and there is a lot of really poor history spouted by talking heads on some of these things, so professionals should be doing it. There's a public dimension to our profession, in my view.

How do you see the battlefields playing into that?

Well, that's another part of it. I have done innumerable tours. I have no idea how many times I have been to Gettysburg. These sites are wonderful interpretative sites and not just for where the 20th Maine was or whether the 4th Texas got 150 yards up Little Round Top, or was it 152 yards? Let's argue about that. There's way too much of that that goes on. But when you get people on those sites they become very receptive to questions like, "Why is the 4th Texas even here? What did they think this was about?" Even the monuments are great teaching tools. "Here's this monument that talks about union, it doesn't talk about emancipation," or the text on the Louisiana and Mississippi monuments from the 1970s—it's just unfiltered, pure Lost Cause.

Battlefields are wonderful educational places; we need to preserve them. With my Civil War courses, I have an optional battlefield tour. The students don't get credit for going. I tell them where I am going to be and if they want to come that's where they should be, and we spend the day walking around.

I assume you have a lot of them show up?

I do, and we go as far as Antietam. The last time we went there we had eighty people who showed up. A lot of them bring friends, family members, fathers, and uncles. Students from past classes show up.

In addition to their value as teaching tools, the battlefields should be preserved because you can't understand the battles unless you go to the ground. I grew up reading Douglas Southall Freeman's writings; I still use them. But the first time I went to the McDowell battlefield from Stonewall Jackson's Valley campaign, it became abundantly clear to me that Freeman had never been near it. How he described the battle had nothing to do with the ground there. You couldn't have written what he wrote if you had been standing on the ground.

What is your opinion of the whole graduate school process of getting a PhD: the comps, the language requirements, the dissertation process?

It's a tradition. You jump through certain hoops. Why? Because you jump through certain hoops. Why did I have to show proficiency in Spanish when I was a graduate student? The answer is because I had to show proficiency in something. What are the chances that I will ever need a language in my work? Zero. So the Europeanist disdain for Americanists has some grounding in that they really do have to have a proficiency that most of us don't have to have. But we still need to learn it because if you have a doctorate, you really should have something more than English as a language.

The comprehensive exams: I think there is something to going through comps.

The comps at Texas were a one-shot trial by fire. There was no written element. It was a three-hour oral and that was it, which was intensely anxiety producing. Students complain about having to take a written and oral component, but I think it's a wonderful hedge against disaster because you can do very well on one and sort of mitigate a bad performance on the other. One of my best friends at Texas went into his orals, and I never saw him again. He had a meltdown, walked out of the room, walked out of the program, left Austin, and none of us ever saw him again. There were several instances of people for whom the orals were the end of the road.

But you managed to do fine.

I managed although I had a horrible initial experience because one of the professors on my committee had forgotten that my orals were that day, and he came bustling in and told Lathrop he would have to go first because he inadvertently scheduled another meeting, which really didn't please Lathrop. And then the first three questions he asked me were about Native Americans in sixteenth- and seventeenth-century New England. He had given me no readings on this. I knew nothing. So I stumbled through that. I saw my life flash before my eyes at first, and I was just wishing that I could crush to atoms this person who was asking me about something he never put on my radar screen. It was just unbelievable.

Once I got on firmer ground it was actually a good experience. There was a lot of talk about bibliography and historiography, which was great for me. I've always had a really good mind for titles and dates and authors and arguments, and so that played to my strength the rest of that day. Lathrop loved bibliography, and he and I really connected in that regard. He was just a master bibliophile. He didn't love books as collectible objects as well as scholarly tools the way I do, but he knew the literature, so it went okay after that.

I think there is something to having that crucible. It's a good way to force people to try to synthesize and focus what they know about whatever body of literature and material they are trying to master. I certainly wouldn't do away with it. I prefer the written and oral model. I think heavily rolling the dice just with the oral really works against people, and that is of course a much more stress-inducing situation than sitting down and having eight hours to write. You have a little wiggle room. I don't think that's a good model when all you do is the oral and not the written, too.

Would you consider dumping the oral and just doing the written?

No, because a lot of our world is oral communication, and I think we need to be able to think on our feet. We need to be able to respond to arguments on the fly. It's not enough to write a wonderful paper. You can't get an A from me if you just write a wonderful paper. You have to engage in the discussion because that's what we do. You really need to be able to do that effectively. I know it's harder for some people, but over the course of a semester I expect people not only to contribute but also sometimes to take the lead. The ability to engage in really useful arguments and critiques orally, that's the skill we have to have, and if someone doesn't have it, they are in the wrong business.

Sometimes in seminar classes, discussions turn into nothing more than just finding out what's wrong with the particular book that we are reading.

That's similar to the fallacy of writing a book review that talks about everything the author didn't do, and it would have been a good book if only it had been written as the reviewer wanted. I just won't put up with that. Every book doesn't have to check every box. That's the easiest and laziest kind of critique to just say a book doesn't deal with all these things. It's harder to engage the argument. If the author overlooked a key piece, then you should hone in on it and be relentless. But if what you are doing is looking at a book and saying it doesn't do all these other things, then that to me is laziness, and in a seminar it should be ruthlessly rooted out.

The other tendency of course is just to be hypercritical of everything. I remind students that I didn't make up my reading lists with the fifteen worst books I can think of for them to tear apart. These books are good books. All books are flawed; all books fail to do some things. But most professors don't assign books because they are bad books, and if an entire discussion of a book is all about what's bad about the book you are missing the point.

Every piece of work is meant to be criticized, but not in the sense of just pounding away with your sledgehammer. I can indulge in a really long rant about this because I think one of the weaknesses of many graduate students is that they consider themselves peers of the people whose work they are critiquing. I don't believe in that either. There is a difference between being a professor and being a graduate student, the difference being that the professors have all of the power. The professor has life-and-death control in terms of students' careers, so it isn't an equal relationship. You are not pals, and you don't just hang out and drink beer and on the first day of class tell them to please call me Gary. I just think it can lead to very difficult situations because I am judging people all along the way. If somebody has failed a set of comps and they have to go, I think it's harder for them to come to terms with that if they think they are my pal. I think it muddies the waters; you have to maintain some distance because you are put into very difficult situations of having to judge students in serious ways that have enormous implications for the rest of their lives.

When you get into a seminar situation, and students begin critiquing things as if they bring to this critique the same body of expertise and experience as the person who wrote that book, you have to make clear that's not the case. Maybe in your dissertation field where you have done a lot of your work and you are dealing with a book that's done a lot of work in that same field, that's different, but mostly students are not peers critiquing peers. The main point is to grasp the principal argument and then, as the semester goes along, talk about how good literature has changed, how the field has changed.

But of course we were little jerks in graduate school. There is that dimension of being a graduate student. It's partly self-defense in this very precarious world where you don't know if you are going to get a job.

We want you to criticize. You have got to have something to say, but you also have to be ready to acknowledge when something is right. I had this epiphany in graduate school in one of my seminars in western history. We read a book everybody in the class was just savaging, and I was thinking, "I really liked this book." They were criticizing it for all the things it didn't do, and I said I thought it did what it set out to do pretty well. They all responded with, "Oh, yes, but he doesn't do this and he doesn't do that." I was thinking that I had completely botched it, but the professor stepped in and supported my position and made an eloquent argument for how a book should be critiqued. I never forgot that. It was my very first semester in graduate school, and it's something that every graduate student should have thrown in their face as early as possible. I do it as a matter of course in the first meeting of every seminar that I have now.

You talked about the importance of being able to communicate orally. When you do have students in your seminar classes who are reserved, how do you address that?

I often arrange to talk to them in my office and tell them that I understand it's clearly harder for them than for some others to get involved, but they do have to get involved. The way to do it is to pick your spots when you get on the ground where you really do have something to say. When your inclination is to be timid, you just have to force yourself to speak up, or you won't do as well in this class as you should. I often say that I can tell from your papers that you are getting the material, and you are able to focus your ideas, and you are able to make your arguments, but you have to take those skills and translate them into an oral skill as well. But if you have been quiet for three weeks, and I want you to talk, I won't point at you and say, "What do you think about this?" I never do that because I think that is counterproductive. You need to find other strategies to bring people into the discussions.

Some people love to talk, and the other side of that is you have to rein some people in who just talk constantly. You have to remind them that the point isn't for me to have seventeen marks indicating comments after your name at the end of a class meeting. What you have to hope is that I walk out of the meeting with a sense that you read the material carefully and made pertinent comments that moved the discussion along.

You also have to make clear to them that counting coup on other members of the seminar will not get them points. There are different cultures in different graduate programs. Some really encourage a kind of scorched-earth, lay waste to everybody else so that you will look better attitude. I absolutely won't tolerate that. That doesn't get you anywhere in my world. I like people who disagree with each other but who do it in a constructive way and not in a way where they are trying to make someone else really look bad.

Do you think there should be some exposure to teaching built into graduate programs?

I do. Students at Virginia get real experience teaching sections. I teach a fairly large undergraduate survey course on American military history. It has TAs, who have three sections of twenty students each. They meet with them one hour a week in a little seminar setting, and I sit in on some of those. The TAs with sections represent one place where students have a chance to teach. We also let some graduate students who present good ideas for courses teach undergraduate colloquia here, so that's a chance for them to have a real course limited to fifteen students where they are responsible for everything. They don't teach survey classes here like they do in a lot of places. If you go to some larger universities, you have thousands of students in survey courses taught by graduate students. It's necessary in some places, but I think that's a problem.

I taught a class at Texas. It was George Forgie's Civil War class—he was on leave—just before I went to Penn State, and I had never taught before. You have to start teaching somewhere. Senior graduate students are in a position to do that, but I think there should be some screening. There are some people who shouldn't be inflicted on students. Either they aren't ready to be inflicted on students or you find out some people just can't teach. We tolerate way too much of that in our profession. There are lots of wretched teachers who have tenure because they publish well. I don't buy this notion that you can do either one or the other. These jobs are so precious and the pool is so large that every position should be filled by somebody who can teach at least competently. You have to be a competent teacher and also a competent scholar. There are plenty of people to go around who meet those two criteria; those should be the baseline criteria. You have to start teaching somewhere, and I think senior graduate students do a lot of very good teaching.

When should graduate students start looking for jobs?

I don't think they should start looking for jobs until the year they are certain they are going to graduate, and often even then they are at a disadvantage because they are up against people who have their degrees or maybe even a book. Departments are wary of people who haven't finished their degree: it's taking a chance that someone will finish. It's such a disadvantage not to have your degree when you start a job because the amount of work is overwhelming if you haven't finished your dissertation, and it really makes it hard to finish it. So I would never have a student go on the market before the year that I am sure they are going to finish. Some choose to wait and do it the next year after they graduate.

It's very hard to keep people's spirits up because there is so much rejection. What you have to get across is that you cannot take rejection personally, because you can have no idea what factors are in play in the hiring process. You can be the best candidate, but there can be a division in the department and one part of the department for whatever reason doesn't like you or maybe doesn't like your advisor, and so they are going to be against you. Anything can be at play; you can't take it personally.

For graduate students who are still trying to find a topic for their dissertation, what kinds of questions do you think southern historians should be asking right now? What directions should the field go in?

I see a lot of good work that moves the scholarship along. I think we are going to see a lot more environmental history. That's something where there is room to do a lot more. I would like to see more work done that genuinely calls on gender and race in a way that makes it part of a broader examination rather than just looking through the lens of gender, or only through the lens of race or class. I think those approaches often lead to distortion. The best kinds of history will address a subject by showing how all of those factors play into a broader picture. I think it is important to not exaggerate the degree to which one or the other plays into a question.

Memory histories have been hot for some time, but I think that trajectory may be starting to fade. I am very interested in it, and I think it has helped us a lot. Cultural history is in the ascendancy in some ways. Even social history is sort of on the wane. We are finding new ways to do political history. I think it is important to pull some of the often deprecated approaches to history, such as diplomatic history, political history, economic history, military history, back into play. Those kinds of things are great engines in the lives of human beings. I think they are out of fashion partly because of the ways they were practiced in the past, but those kinds of history can be done in a way that is attuned to social, cultural, and nontraditional approaches.

I think it is going to be a shame if in ten years history departments look up and all they have are social and cultural historians. There is a tendency to hire what we are in our fields. I think we need everything. True diversity in a department is having diverse approaches. It should be diverse in subjects, diverse in methodologies, diverse in politics. I think students should be exposed to widely different notions about what is going on. Let them fight it out. I hate the party line. We should tolerate all kinds of ideas as long as they result in good scholarship. I don't believe in scholarship by advocacy. I believe in advocacy, but let's not call it scholarship.

Do you think Civil War history is played out?

Of course I don't. It's a more vibrant field now than it's ever been at any other time in my lifetime. The Civil War used to be a fairly narrow field. A fascinating way to look at this is to read Thomas Pressly's *Americans Interpret Their Civil War*, which came out in 1954. Look at what the questions were and look at what the arguments were, and then read the book *Writing the Civil War* that Jim McPherson coedited with Bill Cooper in the late 1990s.[1] You see a sea change in what Civil War history is now. And if another such book were published now, the roster of topics would be significantly different because of the vitality of the field over the past dozen years.

The Civil War is a much bigger tent than it used to be. The part of the tent that deals with religion is still far too small. Across the board, religion should be more important to the academic enterprise than it is. I think that the fact that it's not important to many historians makes us conclude that when people spoke in religious terms it was just boilerplate. Well, why do we assume that? I think that it was important to them. I don't think we do enough of that. The really good books on religion in the Civil War would fit on a very small shelf. The fact that there is so little work done on it, when there has been so much done on the war, is ridiculous. Religion was very important to millions of Americans, and the literature absolutely doesn't reflect it.

How about Civil War military history?

I think some things are played out. Historians have written four hundred pages on the first phase of the fighting on McPherson's Ridge. I mean, we have four hundred pages on the railroad cut; I think that's enough. But military history? I have a more expansive view of military history than do a lot of people. I am editing another series at Chapel Hill, called Military Campaigns of the Civil War. We have essays on leadership and some tactical things, but we also have essays like Jim Marten's in the 1862 Richmond Campaign book that deals with slaves and civilians in the Peninsula campaign. We need to think more broadly and understand there are myriad connections between the home front and the battlefield. You can't separate them and expect to get anywhere; military history is much broader than that. There are still books that need to be published about battles, tactical things. Good tactical history is hard to write, and I appreciate it, but I think we are getting into too much detail about smaller and smaller pieces. I'm not advocating an end to this kind of military writing—just saying that for most students of the war, increasingly detailed tactical studies do not provide much useful help in grasping the larger questions and meanings of the conflict.

Why does history matter to you?

History matters to me on several levels. It is intrinsically interesting to me. I have had a very active imagination about history my whole life. It's better than most fiction in my view. Maybe a part of it was because of my isolation on a farm growing up. There weren't a lot of other kids nearby, so I spent a lot of time reading history.

But I also think history is important because people need to know there's a reason why certain things are in place now, whether it's debates about race or whether it's notions about how strong the central government should be or whether it has to do with foreign policy. There is very little new in my view, just variations on themes.

For example, Americans have criticized the government during the midst of wars before. If people could read comments in Congress during the war with Mexico, or comments in personal letters, or comments from soldiers who were unhappy with what was going on, they would discover that our current situation isn't new. You can criticize the government in the midst of a war; people always have in the United States. If there were some sense of that, I think it would be useful in some of what is going on now in the political discussions of our current war. The shrillness of our debate on both sides I find very off-putting, and part of it is there is this spectacular ignorance about US history. The talking heads are just not informed. They say, "Gosh we have to deal with this, we have never had to deal with this before." Well, yes, we probably have had to deal with it before. Just look back past 1996; you might find we have dealt with all of these things before.

Beyond all of the things you have already said so far, is there any advice that you would give to graduate students out there right now?

The most important piece of advice should be the first piece that any prospective graduate gets: if you are not really on fire about this you should go somewhere else; otherwise you are wasting your time. There are so many graduate students who are on fire about it, and you are not going to compete successfully with them. You really have to take a vow of poverty on the one hand, and a vow that you are willing to be frustrated and humiliated in some ways. The only way that you can do that is if you are so interested in history, in learning about it, in making your contributions to the literature, and telling other people about it, that you simply are not going to be able to do anything else.

I have counseled a lot of graduate students out of programs because they did not have that kind of passion. They really should go because they are breathing air that they shouldn't be breathing. It is a field that is ferociously competitive, and you have to have a bedrock desire to pursue history well in order to make your way. If you don't, you shouldn't do it.

You are going to get a lot of negative input, but you will also get positive input. You need to understand that you are apprentices learning a craft. It's a long process filled with difficulties, but the payoff is so great. There is no better way to spend your life than getting paid to read and write and teach about something that you love. Really, there's nothing else like it.

NOTE

1. James M. McPherson and William J. Cooper Jr., eds., *Writing the Civil War: The Quest to Understand* (Columbia: University of South Carolina Press, 1998).

5

Modesty Goes a Long Way

A Conversation with Richard J. M. Blackett

Blake Scott Ball

Originally from Trinidad and Tobago, Richard J. M. Blackett developed an interest in the study of history as a young man. He pursued a degree in American Studies from the University of Manchester in the United Kingdom, and after earning an MA in 1973 taught US history at the University of Pittsburgh, Indiana University, and the University of Houston, where he was appointed John & Rebecca Moores Professor of History and African American Studies. Currently the Andrew Jackson Professor of History at Vanderbilt University, Blackett continues to teach the history of the abolitionist movement, African American history, and Caribbean history. He has written or edited numerous books, including *Building an Antislavery Wall: Black Americans in the Atlantic Abolitionist Movement, 1830–1860* (Louisiana State University Press, 1983), *Beating against the Barriers: Biographical Essays in Nineteenth-Century Afro-American History* (Louisiana State University Press, 1986), *Thomas Morris Chester: Black Civil War Correspondent* (Da Capo Press, 1989), *Divided Hearts: Britain and the American Civil War* (Louisiana State University Press, 2001), and *Running a Thousand Miles for Freedom: The Escape of William and Ellen Craft from Slavery* (Louisiana State University Press, 1999). His current project examines the conflicting ways in which communities responded to the 1850 Fugitive Slave Law. In addition, Blackett has served as associate editor of the *Journal of American History* and editor of the *Indiana Magazine of History*.

Blackett initially sat down with Blake Ball at the Southern Historical Association's annual meeting in Mobile, Alabama, in November 2012. After an interesting conversation, they discovered that the recording software had not functioned properly. The conversation that follows comes from the second attempt, which took place over the phone later in November. In the conversation, Blackett shares his views about his education and his research, as well as his thoughts on graduate education and—fittingly—the use of the latest technology in the historical profession.

Tell me a little bit about your experience as an undergrad, studying history. Why did you decide to study history in the first place?

Well, I had no other skills. I was pretty good at history in high school. At my high school all we did was humanities and mathematics, you know. We did French, and English, and Spanish, and geography, and history, but there were no sciences in my school. There was no lab. I went to school in Trinidad, so as a result I could have studied law I suppose, but that was something I didn't want to do, so I ended up studying history because I also like to tell stories.

So you intended then to teach? Was it teaching that drew you to the field, or was it—

I don't know. I don't know. I never had those kinds of plans laid out. As an undergraduate I did history, economics, and political science. I suppose I could have gone into the diplomatic service in Trinidad, but that never—it never happened. It was never planned, and it never happened. Once one finishes an undergraduate degree, there is the question, "What am I going to do?" And then you start fumbling around, and somebody suggested I go to graduate school, so I did. It's as simple as that.

And so you were in England at the time for your undergraduate study.

Yes.

And so then from your undergrad, once you decided to go to grad school, you went to Manchester.

Correct.

What was your experience as a graduate student in history at Manchester?

I did it in American Studies. Not in the History Department. I chose American Studies because a person from Manchester who taught in the Department of American Studies—at that time it was probably the best American Studies department in England—came to my undergraduate university to give a lecture, and we started talking after. He suggested that I apply to Manchester, so that's what I did.

And then my purpose was to do a twentieth-century topic. In the British educational system if you do get into what we call postgraduate studies, then you are largely on your own. You meet with your advisor periodically. He or she asks you how well you are doing, and you say what you've been doing, and then you go back to the coffee bar, or the library, or wherever it is, the bar, and you continue doing what you were doing before.

So there isn't much . . . there are no required courses that one has to take. One goes in and from the first day you start doing research on your dissertation. So that basically is it. So my experience as a graduate student is nothing compared to what you guys have to do.

You know there's none of the interminable courses that you have to do. There are no book exams. There are no qualifying exams before you get to work—there is no prospectus on your thesis. You just . . . to some extent you are on your own, with some guidance from your advisor, obviously, but you and your advisor come up with a topic, and it's up to you to go and do the research and write it.

Oh, wow.

And then you present it to the professors, and they say "yea" or "nay."

*[*Laughs.*] So I imagine—*

I don't think I ever gave my advisor a chapter.

Really?

No, when you are finished, you hand it in.

And then they look at this and they say, "Oh, this doesn't pass. You must start over." Or something like that. But fortunately this didn't happen to me.

Thank goodness. Did you know anyone that had that experience? That had it handed back?

Yes. Yes. I've met people subsequently—not while I was in graduate school, but subsequently I met somebody who was on a train while I was going off to do research in London. He had a bound copy of a dissertation in his hand, and I said, "Oh, it's finished." And he said to me, "No, it isn't." And I said, "Oh, dear." He said he was about to meet with the person to tell him that this was not—that this doesn't come up to par, and he has to do some more work, so.

Oh, my goodness. Wow.

Yes, so they were shocked, I suppose.

So while you were doing your dissertation, did you get any opportunities to teach there at Manchester?

No. No, we—well, I did . . . I did my work part-time because I didn't get a fellowship, because as a foreign student you couldn't get a postgraduate fellowship. So I was teaching high school at the time. I was commuting between Manchester and the high school where I was teaching and trying to do the other stuff in between.

I know there are a number of graduate students who find themselves in a similar position of having to teach to make a living while they try to finish a dissertation.

Yes, it's hard. But I never got to the stage of writing a dissertation. I only did an MA thesis because, again, under the English system what happens is that you usually enter the program to do a master's. As they used to do here until very recently. Everybody entered to do a master's, and at the stage of writing your thesis, if you and your advisor think it's worth it, you can then submit the thesis for a PhD dissertation. That's how it used to be done. But you have to fulfill certain residency requirements. That means you have to be in the place for a certain number of years, and by that time I was over in the United States.

And the secretary of the university knew that I wasn't there. So when I wrote to submit my thesis for a PhD, he said, "You didn't fulfill the requirements." So I said, "Could I get the MA waived?" And he said yes. So that's how I got an MA but no PhD. I don't have a PhD.

Graduate students in most programs are led to believe that any meaningful career at the university level naturally requires a PhD. Do you think you are the exception that proves the rule, or is the PhD simply less essential than it is perceived to be?

I am not sure if the requirement of a PhD for life at the university is "natural" as you ask, but it has over the last few decades become standard. I remember my dean at Pittsburgh asking me if I had any intention of pursuing a PhD. Out of sheer cussedness I told him no, but I also knew that a master's degree from a British university still carried some weight. Whether or not I was an exception in 1971, I am surely one now. I can't think of a single colleague who would consider hiring someone without a PhD. Although how they would react to the appointment of an E. P. Thompson or a C. L. R. James [scholars who also never had PhDs] would be interesting.

You mentioned that after coming to the United States you ended up in Pennsylvania.

Yes, the University of Pittsburgh.

So how did you end up in that job at Pittsburgh?

I was working at the Institute of Race Relations in London with somebody who had taught in Pittsburgh, and he knew I was going to America to do research. He said, "Let me put you in contact with some people. You might be able to teach a couple of courses part-time while you're doing your research." And of course this was a great something to fall in my lap. So I said, "Sure." And I took the adjunct spot while doing research. And at the end of the semester the university offered me an instructorship, and I said, "Sure."

So I agreed to do it for two years, and then two years turned into fourteen.

Oh, wow.

Which was one of those fortunate things. Now you don't want to tell any of your fellow graduate students about this because they would think there was a certain element of luck, and I think you're right.

Nobody could have planned this, so I have never—I never had to go through what you will have to go through, which is send out fifty-six applications to jobs all over the country and to go through the agony of waiting for a response. I know. That's a tough one.

I can't offer any advice from that scope personally, because I've never experienced it, although I have had to experience it with all of my graduate students.

But that's the way you have to do it.

Right.

You can't do it like I did.

*Unfortunately. [*Laughs.*]*

No.

When you arrived at Pittsburgh, did anything surprise you in particular about teaching in an American setting?

Well, I don't know if there were many surprises, because I hadn't done it anywhere else.

I had done just high school teaching. So whatever came along I just had to deal with it, but a couple of things surprised me. The size of classes surprised me. Pittsburgh is a large institution with a lot of students, so classes were very large. I mean, as an undergraduate, my classes were always small. One didn't have to go to lectures. One just had to go to tutorials, and then you got eight or nine each in tutorial groups, so it was a much more intimate setting. So these were large classes.

I had to—like you would do, or anybody else who had started their teaching career—keep one step ahead of the students, and I had to spend an enormous amount of time preparing. That's how it is until you get familiar with the course and you teach it; your preparation takes a considerable amount of time.

The students were pretty forthcoming in that they were willing to ask questions. They weren't always prepared for the answer. But, you know, they would ask you questions and you had to respond. And many times if you didn't know the answer, you just had to say, "Look I don't know the answer, but I'll get it to you tomorrow." Or by the time we meet next class.

So it was more a surprise for me than, I think, for the students. So I was learning about how you teach, how you communicate with people, because even after you've gone through all of your training, we don't train people to teach.

And sometimes we give them the opportunity to take a class, or to give a lecture in class, or to teach a course themselves, but really nobody is taught to teach, so you have to do something about it at the beginning, and you have to make sure that you're well prepared, and you have to make sure that you are reasonably vulnerable. Secure in your vulnerability, and you can say, "Look, I don't know the answer to that question." And the teacher's at a disadvantage, you know, because of these confounded laptops. I mean, you say something, and they can check on it right away.

So my advice to people who are getting into teaching is to tell them you don't allow laptops.

For that very reason.

Yes, well, not only for that, but they sit there, and they do emails and YouTube and stuff like that in the middle of your class, so if I allow laptops in my class now they have to sit in the front of the class so I can see what they are doing.

Ah.

They can't sit in the back of the class with their laptop. That doesn't work. Because when I move about and I'm lecturing, then I'll take a peek to see what they're doing. And if they're messing around I put them out of my class. No?

So the students that I encountered at Pittsburgh were the same as students in my generation. Some were there because they were really committed to what they were doing. Some were there because they felt this was what they had to do. Some were there because their parents told them this is what they had to do.

The American undergraduate educational system is much more democratic and much more open, so then there were people of different skills and talents. You just had to deal with that. You know, some people who could write very well, and some people who were not very good writers, and some people who were in between.

And you just have to adjust to that.

Last time we talked to you, you mentioned that you also experienced some difference in the way that American universities do grades.

[*Laughs.*] Yes, yes. I failed my entire first class. Yes. Because when I was an undergraduate 45 was a passing grade. An honorable passing grade. Now if you get a 45 in a class in America, you are somewhere, you're like—you've got a real problem. So before I put in my grades I asked a colleague, and the colleague said, "Well, Richard, you just failed the entire class." But I just had to go back and just had to add some numbers to it.

But you know, as an undergraduate I got a very good degree. I think my highest grade ever was a 70 percent. So it's just a different grading system.

Nobody, nobody, as I can recall as an undergrad, ever got 90, you know? It just didn't happen.

So the grading, that was one of the culture shocks that I had. But I still have a problem—you know, I don't give A+s. I don't know what that is. If A is the ultimate, then that is what you get.

So I don't know what A+ is. A+ is something that is—well, I don't understand that.

So you mentioned that your experience with your advisor as you were working on your thesis was that your advisor was very much hands-off.

Yes.

How has that affected your approach now as an advisor to graduate students?

No, I don't do it that way because I know I'm in a different setting. If I did that my graduate students would be up in arms. You know? You have to hold hands, and be understanding, and be attentive, and pretend you're interested in what they're doing. So it's a much deeper commitment and an investment of time. But then that's just how it's done here. You know you have to read chapters in multiple versions, and you have to send it back, and insist that it comes up to a level that is defensible, because you don't want to be in the situation where I could have been, which is it could have been rejected. So in that sense, it's a safer and a more secure way of doing it, but it requires a lot of investment of time. Energy.

So with your own work, when you were deciding upon a subject for your thesis, or when you've decided on ideas for your subsequent books, what is that process?

Nowadays what one does is, if you're a graduate student you have to come up with a prospectus, and all that sort of stuff, which is to some extent a time-consuming proposition. I prefer a shorter prospectus, or prospectuses, because I don't believe that you have answers to the project that you want to explore until you go into the archives.

Those people who write the interminable prospectus find when they go into the archives that it really doesn't square with what they've chosen, yet they've spent an enormous amount of time preparing it. So I think you have an idea of something that interests you, and you go about seeing whether or not somebody has done this before. And in many cases it's purely chance that you come up with a subject.

I mean, the subject of my first book was the result of where I was in Pittsburgh. There were people who were looking in the early 1970s for some of the origins of black nationalism, and one of the people that we were discussing and latched onto was a man called Martin Delany. Martin Delany went to England and Africa in 1859, 1860.

I usually went back to London every summer because I was married, and I thought, well, I'll see what Delany did when he got to England. Then I discovered in looking at that, that there were lots of other black Americans going to England, so that led me to ask the question, "Well, why had this happened?" And that was the result of my first book. There was no light of great intellectual insight. I was trying to please my wife, and in the process I wrote a book. How is that?

That's not too bad. So it was the product of—

It was marriage and obligation, as they say. And I didn't just want to sit around in England all summer and watch cricket, although that's quite pleasant. So I did. I started doing this research, and then as a result, there's the book.

So there's no great scheme. There's no great intellectual plan. There's no flash of light or genius, there's just—it just happened. You historians like to talk about contingency, right? Well, there's contingency for you!

I often wonder as I'm working on my doctorate, and about to be writing these interminable prospectuses and work on a dissertation, I never imagined a day when I would publish a book. Did you grow up with any sense that one day you were going to write a book, or multiple books, and what was that experience like when you finally published something?

No. The simple answer to that question is no. I had no plans. No idea. No ambition to write a book, because that's that long vision one has to have, and I tend not to operate that way. So no, I didn't plan to write the book. And when the book was finished and it was accepted, and appeared, one of the rude awakenings I had is that it had no effect on the world.

Huh.

Yeah, it's very sobering, you know? Your book comes out, and the world continues to function as though you didn't write a book. Which is damn inconsiderate, if you think about it.

*[*Laughs.*] Wow.*

People should be more sensitive to your accomplishments.

Right.

Nobody stopped me in the road, and the price of coffee did not change. So it keeps you modest. And in this business I am absolutely convinced that modesty goes a long way.

Because we have all these—everybody has a PhD, and things like that. People have a strong sense of entitlement based on what they see in their accomplishments. That always creates potential problems, so you have to be modest. You have to say, "Look."

I mean one of the things that struck me most when I went to the university as an undergraduate is that the first day I was absolutely convinced I did not belong because there were all these people who had infinitely superior grades than I did.

And I was in an educational institution that only admitted fewer than three hundred people the year I was admitted. And what struck me, by the end of the fourth year when I was finished, possibly sixty of them weren't there. So people got expelled as a result for—I mean for academic reasons. They just didn't cut it. And these were all people who were very bright with excellent grades. So you have to keep all of these things in perspective, and you have to keep a sober head on you, and you can't take yourself too seriously. So that should depress the hell out of you.

I've experienced a very similar thing in going through graduate studies myself, having a feeling that there are folks I'm working with who are much smarter than I am. Much more intelligent than I am, but they don't always seem to be the ones who finish the race, so to say.

Oh, that's because this is a race for people who are a little bit dogged.

You know, you just have to do it. There's no mystery to it. People tend to get lost along the way because all kinds of things come into their lives. They can't focus on the matter at hand. All that sort of stuff. So no, you have to be dogged, and you have to wear blinders to some extent in order to finish the project once you've started it.

So yes, there are lots of bright people, sharp people, who don't finish because they can never stop reading the next book. Because they want to be able to engage every issue. As though if they did, the end product would change the course of history. I don't know.

So perhaps there's a degree of perfectionism that stifles them.

Perfectionism to some extent has its strengths, but it can be very debilitating at times because it can consume you, and you lose all sense of proportion because you want to have the last word. And you're going to finish, or need to find out if you still have a lot of work to do, so the dissertation is a stage. It's an important stage, but nonetheless it's a stage. And you can do the magnum opus when you're done. When you're finished with the dissertation.

That's why it takes people so long, to some extent, to finish. Not only because of all the other requirements that take up a lot of your time. But then you have to do all this research, and then questions are being asked of you about whether or not you're coming up with all the right answers. You push yourself to do more, and in the end it seems to just consume you.

Mmm.

Yeah. There are a lot of bright folks who don't finish.

Yeah.

So you can go and cry in your beer.

[Laughs.] In a strange way, though, it's actually encouraging, because as we talked about last week, the steps to succeeding are actually rather simple. It's just a matter of doing it.

Yes, well sometimes that, too, can get to you.

[Laughter.]

Especially when you have to do exams. You see there are all these peaks in your training career. You have to get over these individual courses, then you have to take these interminable exams. And then there's a tendency, a natural tendency, to just let down a little bit. Then you have to do your prospectus. And you're finished with that. Then you have to go into the archives. Then you have to start saying, "What does all of this mean?" So you have these peaks and troughs, and you just have to make those troughs much shallower in order to keep going. So you have to transition from one period to another in as short a time as possible.

Right.

I think that's the secret to finishing. If you're going into your exam and you don't know what you're going to write your dissertation on, I think you're in trouble. And I think exams should be structured in such a way so that when you come out of it you're ready to start doing your research, so you don't need to know what happened with the Second Bank of America if it is not interesting to you. That is not what your work is on. And if you have to teach the antebellum period in a course, you can find out about that later on.

Right. So—

So—I hope you're not doing a dissertation on the Second Bank.

No.

Oh, okay.

No, I study the twentieth century, so we're okay.

Okay.

So talking about comprehensive exams and these things, you've been somewhat of a reformer, first at Pittsburgh and other schools—now at Vanderbilt. You've

kind of come in and challenged the accepted manner of doing these qualifying exams. Could you talk a little bit about that?

Yes, well [*laughs*], "reformer" might be a nice word for it.

*[*Laughter.*]*

No. No—well, I believe that if you are training people—and the American graduate educational system is a system of training—we have to try to teach people to do the things that we do. And the way we do it. We do not write blue books.

This is absurd. What we do is we write essays. We write chapters. We write books. So at this stage what you have to do is start acculturating students to the way we do things. And the way we do things is to write them in essay form in which you address the question in a way in a situation in which you have some flexibility, and some space, and some freedom, and some time to answer the question. So you don't stick somebody in a room and give them a blue book and ask them to write it—to answer a question. *We* never do that after undergraduate. I don't even do that in my undergraduate classes.

I never ask for a blue book. So it seems to me that what we should be doing with graduate students is to get them to do things the way we [do them]—to train them to do things the way we do it. And that requires some freedom and some space to answer important questions. So you should be able to write.

So you think the structure is too rigid?

Yes, that's the whole point. *If* you're going to have these comprehensible qualifying exams you simply have to ask people to demonstrate their knowledge in a way that we demonstrate our knowledge. And there's a difference, which is to write an extended essay or an article, in a format that looks like something that we normally do. We don't write in blue books, so you don't stick somebody in a room and force them to answer a question. That's undergraduate stuff. So I think that we should abandon that way of doing things. And I think in most places once you address this issue, colleagues are not tied—they do the blue book way because that is the way it has always been done, you know?

Mm-hmm.

So you can persuade people that there's a better way to do it, generally.

So you've been pretty successful in getting changes like this implemented?

Yeah. Yeah. At Vanderbilt that's how we do it. People take a take-home exam. They have two weeks to complete their qualifying exams.

Oh, wow.

And of course what it does is it raises the bar, the standard. Because if you have that kind of time, more is expected of you.

You know, you can't come in with some garbage. And if you have bad handwriting as I do—I'm convinced that I passed exams because people couldn't read what I was writing. Of course, if they could've read it they would've said, "Ah, fail this man."

So I mean if you put in a take-home you have the time and you're not under that kind of rigid pressure requirement, then you're expected to do a better piece of work.

So that is the sting in the tail, as well.

Right.

So I think that what we have seen are progressively better qualifying exams.

And some of those questions—did you say you even try to engage material that's even of particular interest to the student?

Yes, well, there are two parts of the exam. There's your subject area. And what we have done is that you have two questions on your subject field. One of them is directly involved—so that you have to show a command of the historiography of the dissertation that you're going to be writing. And the second one is a more general question that spins off and has larger significance for the dissertation subject that you are engaged in. So for instance, if you were doing your dissertation on abolition in the United States, your second question would have something to do with setting that movement in the larger context of other social movements, so you would need to know something about temperance, women's rights, and all those kinds of other things. Conditions that are happening in America in this period, as well as similar movements in other parts of the Americas of the Atlantic World. So you have to show a command of that stuff. And the second part of the exam is whatever your minor field is. So you have to answer four questions.

Oh, okay.

Two on each section, so that, basically, is how it's done.

Okay.

So I mean other people could do it differently, but the point is I think the form in which it's done has to be changed. You have to get away from this.

In your personal work, your own research, have you seen—and I know you've mentioned this is a humbling exercise to publish your material and find that the world moves on seemingly unnoticing—have you seen any effects from your work? Have you seen other people pick up your work and maybe use it in ways that surprised you or challenged the way that you initially conceived of your work?

Well, Blake, I've just been talking about modesty. You want me to talk about how my work just changed the world.

*[***Laughter.***]*

I mean, yes. I started working in an area that nobody had touched before. So at least in that sense it set a bar somewhere, and a number of people have subsequently either taken off or engaged the work, yes. I mean, in that sense, it's satisfying to know that some people come along and say, "Well you didn't quite get it right here, but you got it right there." Whatever it is. Yeah. Because my stuff was always set in a transatlantic context at a time when transatlantic stuff wasn't "sexy."

*[***Laughter.***]*

Now everybody—everybody is international and transatlantic.

[Laughs.] You kind of happened to be ahead of the curve.

Well, I stood on others' shoulders, too. I mean that's what makes this business run. I think that's important. There were other people who were playing around with some of these issues, and I just did it differently. I drew on the experiences of lots of other people.

Do you think your Atlantic World perspective has had a profound impact on your work related to the South?

I suppose it has. To a large extent it is the approach that led me to look at the ways the British reacted to the American Civil War and especially to the Confederacy. But what is at the source of much of my work is the conviction that what happens abroad has a profound effect on what happens here.

So what are you currently working on?

I'm working on this interminable project looking at fugitive slaves. It's a solely US topic. And I'm looking at how communities organized to respond to the 1850 Fugitive Slave Law, and how slaves, by escaping, influenced the debate over the future of slavery. The escapes created problems and tensions between communities and organizers; slavery divides.

So it's a big project. I have a cabinet full of paper because I didn't use the Internet or a computer for my notes. It's printed paper. Lots of trees were cut down to do this.

I think we would be remiss after all the challenges we've had with technology in the course of getting this interview down to not talk a bit about technology in the study of history, and maybe ways that you see that affecting your graduate students positively and maybe negatively as well.

There are ways that this has been obviously beneficial, because when you write it, you know, you don't have to go back and retype the manuscript because you changed one page. So that's a godsend.

But the other things—people have a tendency, understandably, to want to take the easy way out with word searches and other things like that. And I'm a firm believer that you have to put in the time in the archives, and go and read the original stuff, and not just rely on word searches. Word searches can help, but they shouldn't be what drives the research. So for some people, some of my graduate students, I've had to push them into the archives and lock the door.

You know?

I said, "Where did you get this? Explain." "I did a word search." I'd say, "Uh-uh. I don't want to hear it."

And what is the danger of a word-search-based database?

Well, it would be like working—some of my students work from newspapers—when you go to one of these digitized collections you are relying on a number of things. First, the person who has decided what words are the words they are going to highlight. And second, you're relying on this person finding all the necessary and relevant newspapers. It doesn't always work that way. If you're working on a subject that involves ordinary people, like a couple slaves running away, there may only be two lines in the newspaper that nobody picked up. But by you going through the newspaper, in your search you might find this and then that leads to other things that lead to other things. So that you can then follow the trail. And after all this, nothing is more satisfying in this business than the detective work of following trails and seeing where they lead.

So you may have missed that. I've gone up to a number of these folks who are selling these systems, and I ask them something and invariably the word systems don't pick them up, because the person didn't think, whoever was doing this didn't think it might be important. No.

But it can help in other instances, but you also have to put in the time. But after all, given that it can take you six or seven years to come to this dissertation, what is the rush?

Good point.

It's a laid-back kind of profession. Take your time.

So you mean I have to go to the archive and sit in front of the dusty old microfilm machine?

Yes! You can do that or you can have the original paper in your hand [*laughs*]. And then they'll give you gloves. Your white gloves. And a pencil. You have to try to write with a gloved hand. That is not easy. It will make you a better person, Blake.

Yes. Well, if you're like me, I have to take a box of Kleenex as well, from the dust.

Yes. Yes. Yes, indeed. You have to wash your hands when you're done.

Well, let me ask one more question before we finish up. Again, I greatly appreciate your time and your willingness to do this interview twice. What do you see as the historian's role in society? What is our function for the world outside of university walls?

Oh, man. Well, I mean—I don't know. Again, it's one of those things where we have to write—regardless of what it is we write—in a way that people can understand it, and read. Now people love reading history. We tend not to write history in a way that engages people and catches their interest.

You know, we lament the fact that the untrained amateur historians sell all the books. That's because we write sometimes some of the most turgid stuff that's imaginable, because we have to fill this stuff, we have to overlay it with all kinds of serious analytical framework. And so forever I was asked, "What's your analytical framework?" It's like a new religion. I tell them I was raised Catholic.

We have to try and do that. It doesn't always work, so we have to write in such a way . . . it's not to say that analytical stuff and interpretations are not important. They are important, but they do not drive what we do. We must write in such a way that people would read it. And even when we do that, 95 percent of the time they're not going to read it. You know, my kids don't read my books, for heaven's sake. You know?

Can't even find a way to bribe them?

No. Not even my wife reads my books, so . . .

I don't think my wife has read a thing I've done in graduate school either.

I wouldn't worry.

Okay.

Some disciplines—history is less of a culprit here—have just lost all sense of connection. They must talk—they feel an obligation to talk only to one another, so they talk in a patois nobody understands. We do have to write in a way that it reaches people and so that we don't put up unnecessary barriers between ourselves and the public.

6

Making Sense of Patterns
A Conversation with J. Mills Thornton III

Joseph W. Pearson

J. Mills Thornton III was born in Montgomery, Alabama, in 1943. He graduated from Princeton University with high honors in 1966 and received his PhD from Yale University in 1974, writing under the direction of C. Vann Woodward. He joined the Department of History at the University of Michigan in 1974 and spent his entire teaching career there, retiring in 2010. His *Politics and Power in a Slave Society: Alabama, 1800–1860* (Louisiana State University Press, 1978) received the Dunning Prize of the American Historical Association. His *Dividing Lines: Municipal Politics and the Struggle for Civil Rights in Montgomery, Birmingham, and Selma* (University of Alabama Press, 2002) received the Liberty Legacy Prize of the Organization of American Historians. He was a Guggenheim Fellow and a Fellow of the Woodrow Wilson International Center for Scholars, and he held the Pitt Professorship of American History and Institutions at the University of Cambridge in 2007–8.

This interview was conducted at the University of Alabama in July 2011. In this conversation, Thornton discusses how growing up in Alabama influenced his scholarship as he spent his life trying to make sense of patterns in his past and in the scholarship of southern history.

Could you tell us a little bit about your upbringing? You grew up in Alabama, correct?

Yes, Montgomery. I was born in Montgomery on October 27, 1943. I have really lived there all of my life. I went to school in Montgomery through the ninth grade but then I went to the Episcopal High School in Alexandria, Virginia, and was there in the tenth, eleventh, and twelfth grades. Then I went to Princeton as an undergraduate and Yale as a graduate student and as I was completing my dissertation I taught at the University of Illinois at Chicago, from 1971 to 1974. And then in 1974 I completed my dissertation and that same year I was hired at the University of Michigan where I spent my entire teaching career, from 1974 through last year, 2010, when I retired. But throughout that period [1974–2010], every summer we would return to Montgomery, so I never actually broke my ties with Montgomery at any point. In fact, Alabama was the subject of almost all of the things I have written; during the summers I would come home and do research and then write things during the school year.

It struck me that both* Politics and Power in a Slave Society: Alabama, 1800–1860 *and* Dividing Lines: Municipal Politics and the Struggle for Civil Rights in Montgomery, Birmingham, and Selma *really brought you back home.

That is exactly right. To think about it in emotional terms, all of this history was happening all around me when I was a boy, and I was trying to make sense of it and understand its implications. It is a relatively unique thing for a young teenager to have all of the elements of your day-to-day life, and all of the folks you regularly see on the street and so on, also at the same moment being on the national news.

And having commentators in the national press talking about your local life made me very interested in understanding all of that. I would say understanding it in a sort of deeper way. It seems to me that from earliest times, I had a sense of these events as a product of history.

You are talking about the turmoil of the 1950s and 1960s?

Yes.

Now you are from Montgomery, and I have been down there. It is very much a southern city. What I mean by that is there is a sense, almost a cultural sense, of the smell of the past around the place.

That's really right.

Did you grow up with the Civil War or the echoes of memory around you?

Sure. Absolutely. The centennial of the Civil War happened when I was a young man. The years 1961–65 were the centennial of the Civil War.

Were you in Virginia when that was going on?

Right at the beginning, I was there. I was in high school at the time of the reenactment of the inauguration of Jefferson Davis. And the reenactment of the inauguration of Jefferson Davis coincided with the Freedom Rider riots, which were also in 1961, February for Davis and May for the Freedom Riders. All of that was happening during my eleventh-grade year. So absolutely, I had a very strong sense of history surrounding me and history being made before my eyes.

Now who did you read growing up?

You know that is a really good question. I am not sure that I can recover that, but certainly I was reading the newspapers, and they were filled with historical commentary of various kinds. I suppose I was reading local history. This *is* coming back to me. Now I do know that a major impact on me, as a boy, was Charles Grayson Summersell.

The reason for that is he wrote the ninth-grade history of Alabama, which was really my first exposure to intelligent local history.

It was certainly not my first exposure to local history because my grandmother would talk about it and there was this sort of family portrait of local history. It seems to me from earliest times that I had a sense that this was romanticized and that there was a sort of veil that needed to be pierced there. But Summersell's history for schools was a very serious book. I can remember that, under the influence of Frank Owsley, who was at the University of Alabama and would have been a colleague of Summersell, it talked about how few were the number of slaveholders, particularly large slaveholders; it emphasized the importance of the yeomanry in the life of antebellum Alabama, [and] it talked about the rise of conservatism with the Bourbons after the war. I remember a line in it that said to the effect that "Today, no one would want to be called a conservative but at that time, they were proud to be Conservative." Now that, of course, is a line that is time-bound, because he would have written this during the Truman or Eisenhower years. At any rate, Summersell's ninth-grade history played a big role in my intellectual development. I actually think it is a sad thing and a great mistake on the part of the state of Alabama no longer to teach Alabama history in the ninth grade.

It's taught in the fourth grade now, correct?

Yes. In fact, the way it is set up, as I understand it—I may be wrong about this—the first half of American history is taught in the fourth grade and when you get in high school, and get to American history at a deeper level, they only teach the twentieth century. Well, fourth graders are not prepared to understand the meaning of Jeffersonianism and some of the other difficult themes and concepts! So this has been very poorly done. And they junked Alabama history, altogether, and no longer teach it as its own discrete topic, which used to be in the ninth grade. Instead, their idea is to scatter events in Alabama all through American history.

The result of that is that Alabama history as its own set of developments, with its own integrity, no longer is presented. And you learn about Alabama only as if it were simply a reflection of what was going on in Washington or what was going on nationally. Teachers will say, "This not only happened at the broader level but here is an example of it in Alabama." Well, that's not the way to teach a subject with its own integrity and its own discrete logic.

Is the effect of that approach an erosion of civic interest and attachment to the states? Does that erode interest in state, local, or home?

I do believe that. In my own case, this is a really personal story. I *know* that it was my discovery in the ninth grade that Alabama had its own history that could be studied from a scholarly and intellectual perspective, that it was not just a set of stories told by my grandmother, but this was something serious scholars wanted to investigate and understand, that gave me intellectual permission to try to understand it myself. And it validated what was already in the back of my mind, that real history was made right around me by ordinary folks that I encountered every day, making real decisions. So I never had the sense that history was something far away in Washington or New York.

Your work certainly reflects that. You talked a little bit about that before; can you speak a little more about the stories your grandmother would tell you? I understand that your family was in Alabama for quite a long time.

That's right. I think that had something to do with it. Alabama's history was always in some sense also my family's history. Both families came to Alabama near the beginning of statehood and, in fact, even during the Territorial Period many of them were coming. So I always did have that sense of the interweaving of events in my own background with the history around me. But I was not satisfied with that. I wanted to understand certain broader forces—though I do not want to give myself too much credit at the age of fourteen—but nevertheless it is true that I always had a sense that broader forces and deeper developments were at work in the life of the state and that my family was a part of that. You are right, though, in that understanding my family had a great deal of influence in leading me in the direction of trying to make sense of local history.

Now, you went to Princeton and Yale at a very turbulent time in the history of the South and America in general. Did you find that you had to defend the perception of Alabama there?

Not defend, because I was not interested in defending it; in fact I was interested in many respects in criticizing it. But certainly I found an interested audience who wanted to have Alabama explained to them. That is true. At Princeton and at Yale, there were all sorts of guys who really did want to understand Alabama because the focus of the national news was on not only Alabama but the South, particularly the Lower South. So they would ask me. And that encouraged my developing interest in understanding and telling this story because I felt there was an audience who wanted to know—and needed to know—it. In some sense, the guys I encountered in undergraduate college and graduate school were as much afflicted by myths as my grandmother. In different ways, perhaps, but they, too, were viewing Alabama and the South through a veil that needed to be pierced just as my grandmother was, and that, if anything, pushed me on and led me to want to understand this even more. Of course I had a lot of good teachers at Princeton; Jim McPherson was my first teacher, and he was very interested in Alabama, and he encouraged me to understand Alabama. Now McPherson was not very long out of graduate school, and he had studied with Vann Woodward at Johns Hopkins, and he had written a seminar paper for Woodward on the administration of Governor Robert B. Lindsay [1870–72]. Now he was a very important and interesting man. So McPherson, this teacher I admired, was deeply involved in trying to understand this governor of Alabama in the 1870s. That further convinced me that this was something that serious scholars were concerned about and really wanted to know about. My years at Princeton only deepened my understanding of—not my understanding really; my desire to understand local history and to make sense of Alabama. Then, of course, I went on to Yale to study with Woodward, and his interest in the South was deep and broad, and that even further convinced me that this was a career path of which I was confident.

Did McPherson steer you to Vann Woodward, or did you make that choice on your own?

McPherson did steer me toward Woodward. And then Sheldon Hackney, who had just come to Princeton, was also a Woodward student, and he was the professor with whom I had written my senior thesis. [Hackney was also from Alabama.] Both had just finished studying with Woodward, McPherson at Hopkins and Hackney at Yale. So *both* of them did steer me toward Woodward. Then, of course, I had *read* Woodward and *that* attracted me to studying with him.

Tom Watson: Agrarian Rebel was the first book I read.[1] It was the first book he wrote and the first book I read. Not that I had that much sense, but it was the first book I read. And it had an enormous impact on me. Here I will tell you was the genesis of my doctoral dissertation. I am the only one of Woodward's students who moved back into the antebellum period, I think. But that came out of *Tom Watson*. Because if you will think about the first half, it is all about how Tom Watson was situated in a preexisting radical agrarian tradition.

Tom Watson, even as a boy and certainly as a young man, understands himself as the enemy of the industrializers and as the spokesman for the poor farmers. I credit myself with having enough intelligence to say, "Oh gee, if that was true when Tom Watson was a boy, and then if the issue was there, fully formed and being fought out, when Tom Watson was a young man, that means that tradition must have been there all the way back before the Civil War. And if folks went and looked, they would find a radical yeoman tradition back in the antebellum period. A Jacksonian tradition, in other words, that was carried forward."

That is actually what Woodward thought, too, though he never wrote about it. But if you will think about Woodward, not only in *Tom Watson* but also in *Origins of the New South*, he talks repeatedly about the Redeemers as standing in a Whig tradition and the Agrarians standing in a Jacksonian tradition.[2] It's there in his books. So that was the way he thought of the antebellum period. But I will say it was the way no other historian when I was in graduate school talked about the antebellum period. *Every book* we read when I was an undergraduate and when I was a graduate student talked about the antebellum South in terms of a static politics, not of a developing politics; not a politics filled with conflict but a politics that was dominated by the planter elite, in which the yeomanry were sort of passive, if they were mentioned at all in these books of the 1960s. And that was present before Eugene Genovese. Genovese built on it. Genovese set out to explain that, and he explained it through hegemony. And that, then, was what I set out to attack, the Genovesian hegemonic sense of the antebellum South. Now it wasn't that Genovese had created this in his own books. No, he was trying to explain in a more convincing way why this portrait of the antebellum South was present, for instance, in Charles Sydnor's *The Development of Southern Sectionalism*, a book that was written in 1948.[3]

The interesting thing about that is that Sydnor's* Gentleman Freeholders *points to a more active southern polity than these later books suggest.[4]

It does! It really does. But in *The Development of Southern Sectionalism*, I can virtually quote to you what Sydnor says about that. He says that there appears to be on the surface real conflict in the politics of the Jacksonian South, but in fact, it has the hollow sound of a stage duel fought with tin swords. That's what he says. It's not real.

Well, see, if you take *Tom Watson* seriously, that means Jacksonian politics *is* real and it does *not* have the hollow sound of a stage duel, fought with tin swords. No. It has the real ka-ching of a duel fought to the death. And that was what I believed. I understood myself, when I wrote *Politics and*

Power, which was my doctoral dissertation, as attacking not merely Genovese but an entire tradition of which Sydnor was simply the most prominent earlier exponent.

In* Politics and Power, *you write that "Democracy as a form of government is merely a mirror of men." So you attack the idea that democracy will inevitably lead to a more enlightened, better form of government. It merely reflects the people who elect it.

That is exactly what I believe. I mean that is precisely right.

Please tell me if I am right or wrong, and I would love to hear you expound on it, but there is a sense that you reject what I term the slaveocracy, that it was the elite that led these poor people along [to secession]. And this book does not allow that to stand untested. You say, "No, these people pushed this thing."

Exactly, exactly. Not only that, I would go further to say that the planter elite, for much of the antebellum period—this begins to change in the late 1850s, after the collapse of the Whig Party—understood itself as an embattled minority. Far from thinking of themselves as running the government, they mostly think the government is out to get them. Now the majority of them are Whigs and the kind of program they want is a developmental, modernizing program of public schools and railroads and the rise of urban values—see, that's what the planter elite stands for, and that is absolutely *not* what the state government of Alabama stands for. It is a Jacksonian state government. Now the collapse of the Whig Party, in some sense, ripped out the guts of Alabama politics, the organizing principle of the two-party system that had clarified for the yeomanry the nature of this conflict. And so in the late 1850s, you begin to see the rise of a wealthier element within the legislature so that large planters, who are less than 10 percent of the legislature in 1830 and 1840, and not much more than that, even in 1850, are a quarter of the legislature by 1860. That, I think, has to do with the decline of two-party politics. So the collapse of the Whig Party not only liberated radical Free Soilers to become the Republicans in the North but also liberated the planters to depict themselves as spokesmen for an embattled South in a way that would have been impossible at the time when two-party politics clarified the social drama for the mass of the electorate.

So I believe that antebellum southern politics, up until the late 1850s, is about class conflict. It is odd; I have always said that it is an odd irony that

Genovese, who was a Marxist, spent his career denying the presence of class conflict in the antebellum South, while I, though a non-Marxist, devoted myself to emphasizing the significance of class conflict.

And that class conflict does not go away. Even as late as the Winston administration in Alabama [1853–57], it is there.

What was your relationship like with C. Vann Woodward? What did he teach you that carried with you most throughout your career?

I had a *wonderful* relationship with Woodward, and he was one of the greatest men I have ever known. Now that does not come from the fact that he was a forceful classroom presence because he was the opposite of that. He was a very quiet, self-effacing sort of man, gentle, and even shy. So to get things out of him required a personal conversation in his office, and that's where he was really useful to the student. He was really good when you submitted things in writing to him, very good at that stage, and very good at one-to-one conversation in his office, talking about how you could develop projects or the meaning of things. He was very good at that sort of thing. But he was not good in the classroom.

What was it like writing for him?

Well, it was great. I mean he was very fine, and he added to my doctoral committee Michael Holt, whom I did not know. Now Michael Holt was a young guy who had just come to Yale as a junior faculty member. But he worked in the Jacksonian period, and Woodward did not. So Woodward decided that it would be a good thing for Holt to be on this committee, so he put him on there. He didn't ask me, I just found out that Woodward had put him on there. Now the other member, the third member of the dissertation committee, was Howard Lamar, who was a western historian but was from Tuskegee, so he had a strong sense of Alabama, too. Early on there was another guy on the committee named George Wilson Pierson, who wrote the big book on Tocqueville and Beaumont, and he was a wonderful man. It was a great committee. Now Pierson did not stay on very long; he was an elderly man, and he retired shortly thereafter, but he was on the committee at the time of my prelims, so he was one of the examiners at the time of the orals. Then, when he retired, Woodward appointed Holt to replace Pierson. So the committee at the time I completed the dissertation consisted of Woodward, Holt, and Lamar. Now Holt was a great help to me, too, and indeed, I to him; he was much closer to me in age, of course, so that was a much more egalitarian relationship than my relationship with Woodward, which was much more paternal.

So Holt and I could discuss these matters as peers, whereas Woodward's relationship [with me] was much more oracular. He would *pronounce* on what he was thinking about these issues, but not in a way that required me ever to agree with him. You see he never wanted disciples. He wanted colleagues. He wanted you to find your own way. I wrote a little obituary article about Woodward at the time he died, which was published in *Civil War History*, and it genuinely says what I think about Woodward as a teacher. I was very honest in that piece. It is very clear to me that he's not one of those graduate school mentors who expected you to toe a party line or embroider positions that he already had laid out. It wasn't like that; in fact it was quite the contrary. He expected me to go out and figure out all of this stuff on my own. Now he was prepared to comment about it. But he did not demand that I agree with him, just that I take account of criticisms or holes in the argument that were apparent to him, for my own welfare. All of which was true—I certainly did not want to publish something that had holes in it or was not right.

Can you describe your own teaching philosophy? You suggested that Woodward was not very forceful in the classroom and you differed with him on that point.

Well, my own personality is *not* shy and self-effacing; no, I'm a booming kind of guy. That meant I was effective in the undergraduate classroom because undergraduates like more of a showman and a guy who really says funny things and gets them to think about issues in a sort of friendly and humorous kind of way. That was what my undergraduate teaching was like. In graduate teaching, though, I did try to emulate Woodward because I think that he is right and it is very stultifying of a graduate mentor to impose his point of view. Now that does *not* mean you fail to express your point of view, because you do have a point of view, and it's worth clarifying to your students how you think about these issues.

But I always tried very hard not to be too dominating, to try to allow my students to find their own ways. I have been very fortunate to have had a whole string of graduate students whom I have thought very, very highly of and whose work I have admired and learned from. There is no question in my mind that I have learned from students, at least as much as they have learned from me, and probably a good deal more.

When you look back on your career in teaching and writing history, what have you found most rewarding?

I love teaching. In fact, I loved teaching so much that, having retired, I find that I am missing it a lot. I love research. But writing . . . writing is hard for me. I have to push myself to write things down, but I enjoy research, I enjoy figuring things out, I enjoying figuring out patterns in history. And I think that's what the contribution of professional historians is: it is patterns, it is seeing patterns, it's seeing how things interact and interweave to produce events.

Do you think historians have a civic responsibility? What I mean is that history often becomes very politically charged in a lot of debates. Do you think that the academy should stay out of that? What's your own personal view?

Well, in general, I think we should stay out of it. Now I will tell you how I formed this view. I have served as an expert witness in a couple of highly charged trials here in Alabama. I discovered that trying to explain historical events in a complicated way is *not* something anyone involved in a trial is interested in hearing. Now that means the *judge* or either side—the plaintiff or the defendant—don't want complicated answers; they want simple answers. They want to say this political leader did this because of this particular motive and so on. Well the answer is that a political leader almost never does anything because of one particular motive; indeed, he would not be a very successful politician if he were not sensitive to a whole range of issues. And that is true at an even more complex level when you begin talking about legislative bodies, which of course means you are talking about the motives of hundreds of men and women, and certainly if you are talking about the electorate. You see, historians want to offer thick and complicated explanations and controversy requires simple and direct and therefore misleading explanations.

So my own thinking about that is that historians should go off and write history and then they should try to get people to actually *read* their history, which is hard because good history is going to be complex and is not going to offer readers simple or easily understood explanations.

Secession is something people often want a simple answer for. They ask, "Why did these people decide to secede?" They want to know whether it was slavery or states' rights.

Right. Exactly. They also want other kinds of equally simplistic explanations such as "the tariff" or other kinds of things like that. The answer to that is that this is a political culture and all sorts of things that you would not think are at work, were at work. Attitudes toward Roman Catholicism and the Irish are very much at work in the politics of the 1850s, but you never hear anyone bring it up. But they are very much at work. The building of railroads is very much at work. In the politics of the states in the middle 1850s, the dominant issue is state aid to railroads. I tried to show in the *Politics and Power* book the odd sort of way the fight over state aid played into the politics of Alabama in the 1850s, and my student Marty Hershock showed how important railroads were in Michigan's politics in the 1850s, and my student Richard Nation showed how important they were in the politics of Indiana in the 1850s. Michael Holt's first book talks about how important they were in Pennsylvania, and they were was equally important in Georgia during that period. Yet it is a theme of the politics of the 1850s that is almost entirely neglected in any of the books dealing with the coming of the Civil War. Reading them, you would believe that the Kansas Crisis and Lecompton led directly to John Brown and the Civil War. You would never know that all of these fights about railroad aid, Roman Catholics, immigration—that all of that was making the politics as well. You do not see much about it in many of the books on the subject.

Now to segue between discussions of your two books I have one of those false questions of definition. You have written about two seemingly very different topics, moving from the antebellum South to the civil rights era. What sort of historian are you?

Well, I would say I was a southern historian, in the first place, and then I would say I was a political historian. I believe that the folks of my own generation who dismissed politics were largely wrong-headed. Politics in a democracy, when it is properly understood, is creating and summarizing the conflicts and struggles of the society it represents. I think that very often, in ways that are unclear until you begin to look at it, politics *are* formative. I set out in *Dividing Lines* to show that politics, particularly municipal politics, was at the core of the making of the civil rights movement, whereas virtually everything written about the civil rights movement understood it as narrowly social history. That is not to say it was not the product of deep social conflicts; it was. But politics is also the product of deep social conflicts. Politics becomes a path toward understanding the way in which social conflict is expressed and understood. Actually, municipal politics then becomes the key to understanding the civil rights movement. It answers what was, to my mind, a central question of the civil rights movement that never, ever gets asked, precisely because people fail to appreciate the political aspects of it, and that is, "Why did the direct action movement happen in certain cities and not in other cities that are quite comparable?" "Why do you have a civil rights movement in Montgomery, but not in Meridian?" "Why do you have one in Selma, but not in Dothan?" "Why do you have one in Birmingham, but not in some other city?"

You point to a cracking white consensus.

Right. It has to do with the political experience of towns that allows for a moment of transition that makes it seem that, if now we push, things are changing, and we can get our concerns placed on the table. Those are political events that grow out of municipal political cultures. Think about that. Why in the world wouldn't you have a major civil rights movement in Meridian, Mississippi? That is a real question. Another way of doing *Dividing Lines* would be to look at cities where there were no civil rights movements, but of course no one would buy that book. It is a really important question. Jackson has a civil rights movement, Meridian does not. Birmingham has one, Florence does not. I say a "civil rights movement," but a direct action protest movement is what I really mean, reflecting the discontent in the black community. That is the whole question. There is discontent in the black community all over the South, yet it does not always get expressed as direct action.

The interesting thing for me is that Politics and Power *seems to reply to the history you were handed as a boy by your grandmother that you thought was burnished. Can you talk about the genesis of* Dividing Lines*?*

Sure. I mean, it is still doing that for the most part. This is trying to understand—well, it started with Montgomery and I added Birmingham and Selma, for obvious reasons: they are the other two cities with major, direct action movements in Alabama. If I was going to understand Montgomery, I was going to have to understand Birmingham and Selma, too. I mean I wanted to understand the nature of this movement as a whole. That seemed clear to me. But it started with Montgomery, and the first part of the Montgomery section of this book grew out of an article I published in 1980 in the *Alabama Review*. Sarah Woolfolk Wiggins, who is a *dear* friend of mine, was editor of the *Alabama Review* at that time. She agreed to devote an entire issue of the *Review* to this article, which was about the Montgomery bus boycott. This was in July 1980. Now that was only part of the Montgomery section of *Dividing Lines*, which goes on to talk about the consequences of the Freedom Rides and the Freedom Ride riots, all of that.

The political consequences?

Yes. But the social consequences, too.

Would you argue that the two are intrinsically connected?

I *would* argue that, yes. If I might expand on this for a moment, I would say I was trying to understand the politics of the white community and the black community. Some seemed to suggest that blacks did not have politics simply because, in general, they did not vote in elections. Well that, of course, is absurd!

But the divisions, conflicts, and battles within the black community had not been well understood. Consequently, the result was that the black community had not been well understood. Now the divisions within the white community were a little better understood, but not very much better actually. Because of the segregationists' dominance, there is a tendency to think of the white community as monolithically segregationist, and that is false. There have been efforts along the line of debunking that notion—books like Morton Sosna's *In Search of the Silent South*.[5] But the black community: well, part of what happened with the black community was that King emerged as such a mythic figure that the portions of the black community that did not support King, and the conflict within the black community, tended to recede into the background to the point where that anti-King portion of the black community was just as misunderstood and neglected as the non-segregationist part of the white community. [People only remember] the people that were allied with him, like Shuttlesworth in Birmingham, and Reese and Boynton in Selma, and Ralph Abernathy in Montgomery. All of that had to be recaptured and if you didn't do that, you did not have a sense of conflict. So in some sense recapturing the reality of political conflict is what *Dividing Lines* and *Politics and Power* are about. They are both about that. They are both about the idea that this is not a monolithic politics; this is a politics that is working itself out over time. Portraits of the antebellum period tended to the monolithic as did portraits of the civil rights movement—though there was conflict between the segregationists on the one hand and the heroic followers of King on the other hand, but that is just as much a papier-mâché vision of social conflict as the notion of the antebellum South as dominated by the planter elite.

And then I will tell you, I have to say that I am—well, you said I am trying in *Politics and Power* to pierce the veil of my grandmother's myths of the antebellum period. Well, in *Dividing Lines*, I am trying to pierce myths of the civil rights movement as I lived it as a boy. So there's that going on. These are experiences that I lived through, particularly in Montgomery, and I am trying to understand the complexity of these events and not to understand them as a "good guys versus bad guys" kind of story.

Themes of hegemony and inevitability seem to irritate you in both of your works.

Yes. Right. You are absolutely right about that. I was also going to say that Woodward is at work in *Dividing Lines* also. Just as Woodward is at work oddly in *Politics and Power*. Because *Politics and Power* is a movement backward from *Tom Watson*, and that is a true statement, so *Dividing Lines* is a movement forward from *The Strange Career of Jim Crow*. I say this explicitly at the beginning of the book. In fact I began the book talking about Woodward and the conflicts over *Strange Career*, but nobody seems to have paid any attention to that. But I tried to lay it out there. It is absolutely true what Woodward tried to say in *Strange Career*: that segregation is not—segregation as opposed to white supremacy, that is different—but the laws of segregation are not something that has always existed in the South, even something that existed as soon as Reconstruction was over. They are a product of a particular set of political events surrounding the Populist Revolt. They take shape in the decade between 1895 and 1905, and they take shape as a consequence of the Populist Revolt. What I wanted to say in *Dividing Lines* is that just as very local political events produced segregation, very local political events disestablished segregation. The disestablishment of segregation happens through the same local political processes that the creation of segregation happened through. I take *Dividing Lines* to be a sort of sequel at the ending of segregation to *Strange Career* at the beginning of segregation. In that sense, the Woodwardian view of the world is at work in both my antebellum book and my civil rights book, even though Woodward's own scholarship is about the end of the nineteenth century and beginning of the twentieth century. I have not written about that period because he *has* written about it. But certainly I have formed a sense of the patterns of southern history out of his portrait of the South in the years between 1877 and 1915—those are the years that he used in *Origins of the New South*. And the patterns that he saw there, making sense of those patterns, I have tried to extend those logics or use those logics backward and forward. In fact, my very first article, which was a seminar paper I wrote for him, is about Alabama in 1928 and 1929, which is about the period when Alabama very nearly was—and probably, without cheating, would have been—carried by Herbert Hoover in the election against Al Smith in 1928. And the consequence of that, which was the Democratic Party's expulsion of "Cotton Tom" Heflin from the Democratic Party, allowed John Bankhead Jr. to defeat Heflin for the Senate in the general election of 1930. Because Heflin could not run, since he had been expelled from the Democratic Party, he could not run in the Democratic primary, which allowed Bankhead to defeat him. Heflin was forced to run as an Independent, and that was how Heflin was finally ousted from the Senate.

The point of that article is to try to say that though you might think that the radical Jacksonian tradition was not apparent in Alabama politics after the Populist Revolt, you would be wrong, and where it expressed itself in the 1920s was through the Ku Klux Klan. And I wrote this paper for Woodward, and it was a tough pill for Woodward to swallow. He did not like the thought of the Ku Klux Klan being the inheritor of the Populist Revolt. But I think I convinced him because my portrait of the Klan is not like—see, what he would have resented is a Hofstadteresque portrait that would have said that all along there is in Populism this kind of Rightist, prejudiced, anti-Semitic, anti-Catholic undertone to Populism. That is what Richard Hofstadter said in *The American Political Tradition*, and it is the way students of Hofstadter such as Michael Kazin use the term "populist" today.[6] In fact it seems to have taken over, to the point that people like Jean-Marie Le Pen in France and his National Front are now referred to as "populist." Well, they are certainly not like "Sockless Jerry" Simpson. And Woodward kept saying that Populism in the South was radical and Left and its inheritors were by no means Rightists; and so he was prepared not to like my claim that the Klan were the inheritors of Populism one bit. My claim, however, was not to say that the Klan were the inheritors of the Populists because they were anti-Catholic and anti-Semitic, though they certainly were, but to say that actually if you look, you will discover that there was the radical, small-farmer element to the Klan that expressed itself not only in Heflin, who was deeply anti-Catholic but also agrarian, but even more radically in Hugo Black and in Bibb Graves, both of whom were Klansmen and both of them stand in this Populist tradition. That is what I tried to show in that article about the expulsion of Heflin from the Democratic Party in 1929. That came out in the *Alabama Review* in 1968, and that was the very first article I published, because it was a seminar paper I wrote in graduate school.

In some sense, however, even in that 1968 article about Heflin, I was already exploring the idea that there was this radical Jacksonian tradition in southern politics and it does not go away. You find it expressed in figures like Black and Heflin and Bibb Graves. In that sense, as odd as it may seem, an article about the 1920s and about the Klan was prefiguring the doctoral dissertation that I was just going to start on about the 1830s and 1840s, about the Jacksonians. I do absolutely believe that there was a radical, Jacksonian tradition—which preceded Jackson incidentally—because the radicals were present in Alabama in the persons of Gabriel Moore and Israel Pickens and these very early politicians who preceded the rise of Jackson. In some sense, Jackson, when he became a national figure, incorporates conflicts that had been going on at the state level about all sorts of things, things like suffrage reform and constitutional revision, making judgeships elective, those sorts of things.

My position is that radical Jacksonianism preceded the formation of the Democratic Party and it came out of the events surrounding the Panic of 1819. It also came out of the romantic nationalism generated by the War of 1812 and then the Panic of 1819, the widespread economic hardship from the Panic of 1819; and then it was formed into a national party by Andrew Jackson after he got elected president in 1828 by taking these events and expressing them symbolically in the attack on the Second Bank of the United States. That created the national Democratic Party.

Anyway, I believe this radical, yeoman, agrarian tradition—was present with the settlement of the state, it was there throughout the nineteenth century, and way into the twentieth century, all the way up to the civil rights movement. It certainly was embodied in "Big Jim" Folsom in the late 1940s and early 1950s.

Taking on the "Big Mules"?

That's right. You see, the term "Big Mules" comes from Bibb Graves, and he was the Cyclops of the Montgomery Klavern of the Klan, but he was the radical anti-"Big Mule" guy. The pro-"Big Mule" element was people like Frank Dixon. They wee the people who were his enemies, and they became the Dixiecrats. That was all present in the politics of the 1920s, and into the

1930s, and on into the 1940s. In some sense, it had to play itself out fully in George Wallace. Wallace started off in the radical, agrarian Folsomite tradition and then he directed—redirected it, you might say—in a Hofstadter-esque direction. And that had to do with his longing for national office and his discovery that he could get all of these voters' attention in places like Milwaukee and Indianapolis.

Do you think the crowds Wallace drew in these rust-belt cities in the North get overlooked?

Yes. That's right. That is where a lot of it came from. That, and his discovery that he could tell them how low property taxes were in Alabama and he could exploit their resentments against affirmative action hiring in the steel plants and auto plants and so on. That was directing this radical tradition in a direction that Hofstadter would have understood. Now when Hofstadter wrote about Populism, what was dominating American politics, at that time, was Joseph McCarthy.

So you're saying that is where Hofstadter thinks this "paranoid style" comes from?

Right. He understands Joseph McCarthy as the heir of William Jennings Bryan. Then you see in Michael Kazin's work that exact same depiction. But down here in Alabama that was not the case at all. The populism of Reuben F. Kolb produced Hugo Black and Jim Folsom. It produced a radical, Left tradition. It was itself Left-leaning and radical. I never dissented from Woodward's notions of Populism as a radical prefiguring of the New Deal. No, I always agreed on that point. My position was sort of a median between Hofstadter and Woodward—which was that in the 1920s, the Ku Klux Klan carried on this radical tradition and mobilized the electorate behind Hugo Black and Bibb Graves.

Which gave Wallace a forum to try to carry this tradition toward the Right?

Yes, Wallace helped carry this radical tradition toward the Right.

I have a question about both of these books. I hope I am not drifting toward the glaringly obvious here, but locality, the importance of the local, is a big theme in both of them. How did you come to that seemingly simple point?

Well, I think it is exactly what we have already talked about. It was that I was growing up in a town where national history was occurring all around me. When I was a boy, it was not at all a strange or odd thing to see Martin Luther King or Ralph Abernathy walking down the sidewalk. I mean the events in my hometown were on the national nightly news. Every night.

Even London newspapers were sending correspondents to Montgomery to try to understand it. It was very clear to me that the world was being changed by folks I passed on the sidewalk every day; being changed from all directions; being changed by business associates of my father in the white community [and by] black friends of our cook, walking in the bus boycott. I remember our cook, Lucy Johnson, waiting for the Montgomery Improvement Association carpool car to come around to pick her up at the corner up by our house, as part of the bus boycott. It was no stretch for me to believe that the local produced the national.

Do you like one book more than the other?

No, I like them both. And I like the various articles I have written. As I told you, writing is hard for me. I spend a lot of time thinking about it, and I am not willing to release it until it is good. What I am working on now is something on early Reconstruction and Civil War politics—in Alabama, of course.

It is already an article about the Presidential Reconstruction legislature, the legislature of 1865–67, and the controversy over the ratification of the Thirteenth and Fourteenth Amendments. The Thirteenth Amendment they did ratify; the Fourteenth Amendment they rejected. You won't be surprised to know that when I went and looked at the voting in the Presidential Reconstruction legislature, I found that there was a sharp division between former large slaveholders and former small slaveholders or nonslaveholders. The divisions played out across a whole range of things. They had to redo the tax system because most of the revenue had come from the tax on slaves. That's how you can tell that the yeomanry was powerful in state politics—they *taxed* the planters. And anyway when slavery was abolished, then the Presidential Reconstruction legislature had to figure out some new tax system. And there were big fights in the legislature over that. Initially, what the planters pushed for was a tax on moonshine! Because that was going to be on the yeomanry up in the hills! They pushed for a big tax on moonshine, and they enacted it in the session of 1865, and then in the session of 1866 they had to repeal it because there is such a massive outpouring of hostility on the part of the white, poor-farmer electorate.

What I tried to show is that in the Presidential Reconstruction legislature, the yeoman-planter division is as stark and powerful as it ever was, and it played out in fights over what to do with the freedmen, and it plays out in whether to ratify the Fourteenth Amendment and whether to amend the Constitution of 1865 to allow literate blacks to vote. That's what this article is about. Here again, I think it is because folks haven't looked, because you could not miss these divisions, because they are stark divisions, if you had ever opened the Journals for the House and the Senate for the sessions of 1865 and 1866. I just don't think serious historians have ever looked at this.

You mentioned that now that you are retired, you miss teaching; do you think you will continue to write and research?

Absolutely! I mean, I do that all the time. It wouldn't surprise me if this Reconstruction interest eventuates into something larger. But what I'm thinking about right now is pushing it backward into the Civil War, because I believe that this movement toward poorer membership in the state legislature doesn't actually begin in 1865 but in 1863. It begins in the legislature in 1863. I think I'm going to find that the Confederate general election of 1863 produced a very substantial influx of quite poor representatives, who are playing on massive popular discontent with the administration of the war effort by the government in Richmond. One of the elements of American history that has been much neglected is the Confederate general election of 1863. There's plenty about the Union general election, Lincoln/McClellan [1864], but nobody has studied the election that happened in the Confederacy. Which is, if possible, even more astonishing, that in the middle of a war with an invading army all around, that they hold a general election. But they do. And it produced massive changes in the congress in Richmond. The second Confederate congress was very different in terms of personnel from the first Confederate congress. The president was not up, you know. The president under the Confederate constitution had a single six-year term. So, with Davis, the presidential term would not have expired until 1867.

His administration was effectively on trial at the polls.

It was. It was. And it lost. And then down at the state level, I mean, here John Gill Shorter was defeated for governor by Thomas H. Watts and the state legislature was transformed. So I'm going to go look at that. That's my next project. And then I think I can show that there is a real continuity between the second Confederate legislature and the Presidential Reconstruction legislature. I think I can show that there is an important continuity from then on to the formation of the Republican Party in the radical period.

So you think this might evolve possibly into a book?

I think it might. I have also toyed with the idea of writing a general history of Alabama, under the influence of Charles Grayson Summersell. I think the state could do with a serious history—a monograph that attempts to explain the patterns of the state's social and political evolution.

I'm guessing radical agrarian yeomanry would be in there.

Well, that's what I want to do. I want to explain that, and then I would go certainly beyond Wallace, because I want to show the eventual triumph of the Republican Party. So what I think the natural ending place is, is the final Republican takeover of the state legislature, which just happened. Because that's an extraordinary thing, because now the legislature was overwhelmingly Republican in both houses, for the first time since 1872. I mean, that's a big change.

Much of the commentary saw it in national terms, as part of this Republican triumph in the congressional elections and in other state elections, with the Republicans taking over in Michigan and taking over in Wisconsin, and so on. And therefore it failed to understand the indigenous quality to this change. And you can well imagine that it is this intrinsic change in the indigenous patterns of Alabama political life and political culture that seems to me to be the crucial thing. I think it is a working out of the changes produced in Alabama politics by Wallace. That would be the final chapter of this book, if I ever write it.

I hope you do. Can I ask you a philosophical question just to wrap up here? You've written in and deeply care about political history. In your judgment, what are the prospects of continuing to work in political history? What do you think of that as far as the twenty-first century?

The salvation of political history will lie in paying attention to the roots of political history and paying attention to the way in which politics is mobilizing and expressing the concerns of the electorate. Political history can respond to the concerns of the social historians if you are talking about the way in which politics mobilizes and expresses the concerns of ordinary folks at the local level. Then political history and social history actually become the same thing. There would have been a time not very long ago when the civil rights movement would have been understood entirely as an event of social history. I was writing *Dividing Lines* to show that if you don't understand it through a political lens, you are failing to understand an essential element of its components.

You've located the nitty-gritty politics within this broad, social unrest.

Yes. Or vice versa. The politics is making the social unrest. I mean, the social unrest makes the politics, the politics forms and gives symbolic representation to the social unrest. I think that that is true, all true, of American history. I can't stand this new category of historian that network television has created called the "presidential historian." There is no such thing as a "presidential historian." History departments don't hire a guy to be their "presidential historian." That is not a field, and it shouldn't be a field, because a president, if he is a successful politician—and by definition he is a successful politician—is a guy who is concerned about listening to the people and being at one with the people, and expressing and representing the people. For good or ill, because you started off by saying, and I believe, that democracy is simply the expression of people and we're not all good. I'm certainly not all good, and people all around us are not all good. But politics, when it succeeds, does represent what people wish, and it's better that it does. It's better that they work out their own salvation. At the end of confession in the Roman Catholic Church, the priest says, "Go, and work out your salvation with diligence." And that's what democracy is about. It doesn't give you your salvation. It's about working out your salvation with diligence. And unless we work our way through to our salvation, then it isn't genuine anyway. It is imposed upon you, and it won't work. It won't last. So, in some sense, the story of Alabama is the story of the effort of its people trying to work out their salvation with diligence. And I think that's a moving story.

NOTES

1. C. Vann Woodward, *Tom Watson: Agrarian Rebel* (New York: Macmillan, 1938).

2. C. Vann Woodward, *Origins of the New South, 1877–1913* (Baton Rouge: Louisiana State University Press, 1951).

3. Charles S. Sydnor, *The Development of Southern Sectionalism, 1819–1848* (Baton Rouge: Louisiana State University Press, 1948).

4. Charles S. Sydnor, *Gentlemen Freeholders: Political Practices in Washington's Virginia* (Chapel Hill: University of North Carolina Press, 1952).

5. Morton Sosna, *In Search of the Silent South: Southern Liberals and the Race Issue* (New York: Columbia University Press, 1977).

6. Richard Hofstadter, *The American Political Tradition and the Men Who Made It* (New York: A. A. Knopf, 1948).

7

The Fullest Understanding We Can Muster

A Conversation with Dan T. Carter

Michael W. Mansfield

A native of South Carolina, Dan T. Carter graduated from the University of South Carolina in 1962 and completed his graduate work in history at the University of Wisconsin (MA, 1964) and the University of North Carolina (PhD, 1967). Formerly the Kenan University Professor at Emory University in Atlanta, Georgia, Carter was appointed the first Educational Foundation University Professor at the University of South Carolina in 2004, where he remained until his retirement in 2007. He has also been a professor and visiting scholar at five other institutions including the University of Maryland, the University of Wisconsin, London's Westminster University, Cambridge University, and the University of Genoa. Carter's *Scottsboro: A Tragedy of the American South* (Louisiana State University Press) was awarded the Bancroft Prize in 1970, and he is the author of *When the War Was Over: The Failure of Self-Reconstruction in the South, 1865–1867* (Louisiana State University Press, 1985), *George Wallace, Richard Nixon, and the Transformation of American Politics* (Markham Press Fund, 1992), *The Politics of Rage: George Wallace, the Origins of the New Conservatism, and the Transformaiton of American Politics* (Simon and Schuster, 1995), and *From George Wallace to Newt Gingrich: Race in the Conservative Counterrevolution, 1963–1994* (Louisiana State University Press, 1996). In addition to these accomplishments, he is a past president of the Southern Historical Association.

This interview was conducted in Brevard, North Carolina, on December 19, 2005, at Carter's home (which he describes as the "house that Wallace built"). Carter discusses race in southern history and the importance of understanding the subjects of history as much as possible.

Tell me about your childhood.

I grew up on a tobacco farm about ten miles south of Florence, South Carolina, on the same farm that my family had lived on since the nineteenth century—part of it even back to the eighteenth century. After my father and mother married in the early 1930s, he struggled to keep the farm going, but—thanks to the Works Project Administration—he got a job as a carpenter in 1935. In the late 1930s, he went into the home construction business with a partner. So I enjoyed a split life growing up—raising cattle and growing tobacco, cotton, and everything else on a 250-acre farm. But my father also had a construction business, so I worked in construction as well as working on the farm.

I'm assuming that you were raised in the church?

Oh yes . . . my mother wrote the two-hundred-year history of her Baptist church. I grew up in the Elim Baptist Church, baptized—not many people can say this anymore—in Lynch's Creek. None of this baptistry stuff for me.

They say that a creek baptism puts you closer to God.

That's right. Although I watched one baptism—not my church—in which one guy went immediately to God because, despite warnings, the preacher stepped into the curve of the river, where it dropped off. Both of them disappeared. While the preacher came up, the sinner never did.

It was quite terrifying at the time. The only question that everybody wanted to know was whether he was saved or not. He hadn't come back up yet, so nobody really knew what to make of it.

It has been said that you really can't know the South without first understanding its religion. Do you agree with that?

Oh, yes. I have certainly chosen a different road from my childhood, growing up in the Baptist Church. Later, I was fairly active in the Presbyterian Church, which is moderately unusual for academics, I think. But at that time my children were small, so life in the church came naturally. And then more recently, my wife and I have been active in the Unitarian Church here in Brevard, North Carolina. While it's a different church experience from my youth, you can't get away from it. It's a different kind of religion, but it is still the same thing. And I absolutely believe this, that teaching—less so at a place like Emory, but especially at South Carolina, where I teach now—I think that I have a background that allows me to understand a lot of students and where they are coming from in terms of their own religious beliefs. I think that it is interesting that when I teach southern history and southern culture, the one area in which I am always guaranteed to get a passionate involvement from my students—which can be rare—is when we discuss southern religion. You end up with this passionate involvement with the issues in a way that is totally missing when you talk about politics, or economics, the political economy, or whatever. I never have had to break up a fistfight or anything like that, but it does spur a discussion.

Having grown up in the South, particularly during the 1950s, you could not have escaped the question of race. What was it like growing up at that time, or better yet, when did you first realize the futility of segregation? Does any particular experience stand out?

Well, I don't remember being conscious about it, as I lived in a culture where race was everywhere and yet somehow invisible, particularly when I was young. I simply wasn't very self-reflective about it. I mean race was everywhere, but I never thought about it as such. I grew up on a farm where I knew black kids and played with them, particularly when I was small. There were no black kids on our farm, but there were on my friends' farms. And there is that old thought that race is not as critical [for white people] until you reach puberty. So when you're seven, or eight, or nine, it's a little less powerful and potent, particularly for boys. I played baseball with black kids, or whatever. But all of that ended when I was twelve or thirteen years old. I was fourteen when *Brown v. Board of Education* happened. So maybe it was a coming together of both the fact that I was no longer a young boy and the fact that *Brown* made [white] people far more conscious of race than they had ever been before. It had always been there, but finally you were very aware of it.

There were moments when you were certainly aware of race. I think that it is striking how many southern whites and blacks who are my age remember some confrontation or some moment involving public transportation. In my case, my most vivid memory of race and what a powerful issue it was came in 1952 when I took the bus to Charleston to visit my aunt and uncle. Greyhound, back then, picked up passengers from the roadside. You simply waved a handkerchief at the bus stop and the bus would stop to pick you up. At one stop, an elderly black lady put a young black girl—she must have been eight or nine years old—on the bus, paying the fifty cents or so it took to get her to Moncks Corner, or whatever the next town down the line was. I don't think that she had ever been on a bus before because she sat on the front seat, a big "no-no" at that time. Although the driver didn't even notice her at first, I was very aware of it—it's interesting, I say that you were never aware of race, but I knew that as soon as she sat down that this was out of place. I, of course, didn't say anything. The driver finally realized—he looked up in his mirror and told her to move back. Well, either she didn't understand him or she was simply frightened, because she didn't do anything. He said it again. He barked at her. Again she didn't do anything. Then he slammed on the brakes, pulled the bus to the side of road. Jumped up . . . this was a big man. He leaned over her and yelled at her, "I told you to move to the back of the bus!" She sat there, paralyzed, and started crying. This old black man got up from the back of the bus—the only black person out the half dozen or so of us on the bus—came forward and said, "Come on back, honey," and took her back to the back. And I was just horrified—not about the segregation but about how mean the driver was. I talked to my mother about it, how mean that he was, how cruel he was to her, and that he wasn't polite to her. But it was less about the segregation than about the cruelty of it, that he would be so abusive to this nine-year-old child. And there were other examples of that, where you saw glimpses of it, and you realized how potent of an issue that race was. But growing up in that culture you certainly never looked at it critically.

This is not to say that everybody felt that way. There were those in my community who held different views. My mother had a cousin who was a teacher. I remember that whenever the issue of race came up, he would get up and leave the room. Later on we talked about it; he explained that it was because he had to live in this community. He had served in the army during a segregated period, and he had dealt with black people in a different way, going away to school and all that. But he didn't feel free to say that, so he just simply blocked it out, by not talking, getting up and leaving whenever he could. I had a cousin, James, who had been in the navy during World War II. He was the first person who ever actually confronted me about race because I had started talking about some disturbance in Florence and had used the "n" word. James just stopped me and said that he been in the Seabees during the war, and while they had segregated units and black labor battalions, they had all worked together. On Tarawa he had caught dysentery and thought that he was going to die. They had just arrived and didn't have medical facilities but two of his black buddies looked out for him for about a week. After that he swore that when he left the navy, he was never going to use that word again. And he said that I was too young—I was about fifteen at the time—to understand that the way people feel about black people was a kind of sickness. They simply blamed everything on the "colored" people, covering up their own shortcomings by pointing their fingers at somebody else. This was so shocking to me, because this was a person who was southern, a relative, who, despite having grown up in rural South Carolina, had a totally different way of looking at race.

So did that conversation change you?

Well, I would like to think that I thought about it, mainly because I worshiped James. I thought that he was a great adventurer who had sailed the Caribbean. So I'm sure that in the back of my mind that I was embarrassed. I didn't really change, however, I don't think, until later, when I was working as a newspaper reporter when I was in college.

Was that in Florence?

Yes. Once I graduated from high school I went to an extension of the University of South Carolina. I took night courses and worked at the *Florence Morning News* from 1958 to the summer of 1960.

Is that what brought you around? That's not a good way of phrasing it, I know, but . . .

Understood. I think that it was a combination of factors. The people whom I worked with at the newspaper were quite open, I think, about race, and the teachers who taught at the university certainly were. They didn't go around crusading about it but they were pretty clear that they thought segregation was a bunch of nonsense. There were people my age who went through the same experiences and didn't change their views at all. There were different sets of circumstances. Part of it was that my family didn't talk about race very much. Some southern families talked about that stuff all the time but we just didn't. It was avoidance as much as anything else. My mother emphasized the golden rule, and I certainly never heard her use the "n" word or anything like that. I never heard her make any critical comments about black folks, and, in fact, she often spoke positively about black individuals whom she dealt with, either on the farm or whatever. So I think that I was lucky enough not to have this whole background ingrained in me that black people are threatening or that they weren't as smart. I don't mean that I hadn't picked up some of that nonsense—I'm sure that I picked up some of it during my youth—but it wasn't as big of a break as it was to other folks.

But you eventually graduated from the main campus at Columbia. Was that a factor?

Yes, at Columbia I almost immediately fell into a bunch of rabble-rousers, so to speak. Actually, I've often thought about it. It was a kind of genteel—and certainly not a subversive—program of drawing in students. I've often thought of it as kind of parallel to what the Communist Party's operatives must have done during the 1930s in Cambridge, England, wherever they saw these young people whom they knew were sympathetic. At Columbia I fell in with people—Alice Spearman, the head of the South Carolina Council on Human Relations, and Libby Ledeen of the university's YMCA, and Mae Gautier, who was a young Methodist chaplain on campus—who created opportunities and encouraged you to take part in activities that were critical, for the first time, for bringing you into contact with black students, an experience that was totally new to me. I mean I had, as a newspaper reporter, interviewed young black students who had been involved in the sit-ins in Florence and other places, but I had never been in any kind of social situation in which we were on a level of equality. And that was certainly what Alice and others did: set up meetings, first evening meetings, then we had weekend conferences in which students would come together from all over South Carolina, from black and white schools, and have discussions about race relations or politics. Mostly about race relations because that was the big issue for us. And that was the transformative experience, I think, for a lot of white students like myself. I don't think that it was as significant for black students, but I'm sure that it may have had some impact.

There were also a number of other individuals who reinforced my views. I was in an apartment with Charles Joyner, the author of *Down by the Riverside*, and Selden Smith, who taught for many years at Columbia College, and Hayes Mizzell, who was a civil rights activist during the 1960s—who were all native South Carolinians, like myself, and were involved in civil rights activities.[1] We also shared an interest in regional African American history.

What did your parents think about your activities?

Again, avoidance is a nice southern thing. They certainly never tried to discourage me in any way. I know that in 1960 or 1961, a state law enforcement official came to see my father because I had been at a meeting at Benedict College, the black Baptist school in Columbia. I was driving a car registered in my mother's name—it was my car, but I had never bothered to change the registration—but what I didn't know was that they were photographing all the cars leaving the meeting. So an agent of the State Law Enforcement Division came to see my father in Florence to inform him that his son was attending a "radical" meeting. He may have said Communist meetings, but I'm sure that he used the "n" word as a bunch of black people had attended as well. It's interesting but I never knew anything about this until later. It was my father's secretary who finally told me. She said that my dad told them that his son was old enough to make his own decisions and that it wasn't any of this guy's business. I'm sure that it unnerved him because at that time these weren't my father's views, but he was a great believer in allowing my sister and me to do our own thing, and he never tried to tell us otherwise. I mean, he had always hoped that I was going to come into the building business with him, but when I told him that I wanted to go to graduate school to become a historian, his response was that, first, I needed to do whatever it was that I thought that I was good at, and second, whatever was going to make me happy. I remember being tremendously relieved that there was no attempt to lay a guilt trip on me that I wasn't going to end up being a building contractor for the rest of my life. I would have probably been richer, but. . . .

Maybe you should have taken that advice. After graduating from the University of South Carolina, you went to Wisconsin. That had to be a culture shock. Does any particular instance stand out?

I think that I might have been lucky arriving in 1962. The civil rights movement was just catching steam. I certainly didn't go around proclaiming this, but I think that most people assumed that the two or three southerners around were clearly interested in African American history, although we certainly didn't call it that, and I think that most of the students regarded us as a little exotic. Not in any hostile way at all, as I still have many friends even today from my time at Wisconsin. My greatest concern was my terror that I couldn't compete. I mean I shared an apartment with two guys from Harvard. Most of the other students in graduate school were from far more prestigious schools than South Carolina. I'm not sure that they had better backgrounds than I did, but I certainly felt that they did at the time. As a result, I just about killed myself the first year trying to prove that I was capable of doing the work. And I discovered that after a semester or so that I could do it, that I wasn't at all disadvantaged. But I certainly felt insecure at the beginning. And it was culture shock. It was an odd, odd situation to go from South Carolina to Madison, Wisconsin—I didn't know a soul. I drove up there during the late summer of 1962 in my old Chevy with everything that I could pack into it. I checked into an old downtown hotel with no place to live and not knowing anybody. It was a little odd, but it was a great experience nonetheless. And I would have stayed if my advisor hadn't died.

Who was that?

William Hesseltine. He had been at South Carolina on a visiting appointment. Because of that, Wisconsin was one my top three choices. I was a Woodrow Wilson Fellow, so I could get in anywhere, but it made it easier. My other choice was work with George Tindall at the University of North Carolina, but he was going to be at Princeton during 1962 and 1963. When I found that out, I thought, well, I ought to go to Wisconsin because I didn't want to spend my first year without my advisor being there. Then when Hesseltine died at the beginning of my second year—I had just started writing my master's thesis—I looked elsewhere. I just didn't feel comfortable at Madison anymore. Dick Current was going to direct my thesis, but he had too many students. He was a lovely man, but I just thought that I wanted to go to North Carolina. I talked to Dr. Avery Craven about it, and he said, "Let me see what I can do." Dr. Craven was visiting Wisconsin during my second year at Madison and had been visiting at South Carolina my senior year. I took his course even though I was an undergraduate, and we had gotten along really well. He called me the next night and said for me to call Fletcher Green, who was the chair of the History Department at Chapel Hill. He assured Green that I was a good student, and while I later heard horror stories about Dr. Green, about how stiff, formal, and even unfriendly he could be to graduate students, he was extremely kind to me, saying that we could work something out if I wanted to go to Chapel Hill. He said send him my transcripts next week, or something like that. Can you imagine the casualness of the whole thing? I had just met my wife—she was in Wisconsin doing a master's in speech therapy—and we had decided to get married. It was a very smooth transition going from one place to the other. And I'm glad that it happened that way. It's not something that everybody should do, but to me doing a master's at Wisconsin introduced me to a whole set of people, different ways of teaching, different scholars—Merrill Jensen, David Shannon, and, of course, Hesseltine. And then I went to Chapel Hill and met a totally different set of people, which, I think, was a great way of training to be a historian.

How was it, coming home to the South?

Well, it was an interesting time. Chapel Hill in 1964 had a great faculty, and the community was right in the middle of the civil rights movement. While I was always sympathetic, sometimes attending demonstrations, I simply did not have the time to be involved as I had been when I was an undergraduate. I was married and working very hard on my dissertation. When I got to Chapel Hill with a master's, I was intent on getting out of there in three years, which I was able to do. So I didn't have as much time to really get involved in activities at North Carolina. But it was a marvelous experience.

So let me get this straight—you finished your PhD in three years? That was pretty fast.

The really fast part was—and I say this with some hesitation because I don't want it to mark me for the rest of my life—I started the work on my dissertation on the Scottsboro case in the spring of 1966, just as soon as I finished my course work. I was, at that time, taking my exams, but I had already started doing background research. During the summer of 1966, I really got into it, spending the summer going to a lot of archives. My wife went with me, and she was really helpful—this was a time when it wasn't considered demeaning for your wife to help you. She may just have wanted to get me through. Whatever her motivation, she traveled with me to most places. We had two portable typewriters and we would go into these archives, and I would frantically go through the records. She knew exactly what I was doing so we both went through a lot of notes, handing things back and forth, typing notes. We covered a lot of archives that summer. And then I spent the rest of 1966 and into 1967 doing the research. I spent a lot of time in Montgomery at the state archives. Gosh, we stayed in a lot of ratty places. I've blocked many of them out of my mind. Anyway, it was March before I started writing—March 1967. I wrote five hundred pages in the months of March, April, and May. And it was something that will never happen again, certainly not in my lifetime. You don't get that chance when you're teaching and everything else. I was totally immersed in the story, and it was one of those stories that I just sat down at my IBM Selectric—my parents had given it to us to replace our old typewriters—and wrote up to fifteen pages a day. Spread my notes out, read them, and while I didn't work directly from my notes, I would read them very carefully and then sit there and write fifteen pages. It was a transition in my life—I mean, we all go through it in this field. Xeroxes were very expensive in those days, so I Xeroxed little. I did use a lot of trial transcripts and everything, but I had a 35mm camera that I would set up and take 35mm film copies of critical materials. I would then have it developed for use on a microfilm reader. But most of it was note taking. I sat down with a portable typewriter and took page after page of notes.

I've read somewhere that George Tindall was the one who suggested the Scottsboro Boys to you as your dissertation topic. How was he as a dissertation director?

Well, I had a couple of false starts on other topics, one of which I had already done quite a bit of work on. It was a seminar paper, and I was well into the research when I discovered that Bill Cooper was working on the same thing: the conservative regime in South Carolina. He was at Johns Hopkins then, I think, working with David Donald. So I had to drop that. Then I was going to work on another topic that I later found another historian was already working on. So I was pretty desperate by then and went to see George with my problems. I don't think that I wept or anything like that, but I was pretty frantic. He said that he had a topic, a good topic that was a little contemporary and that he didn't know how much that I could find concerning sources and everything. He then gave me a draft to read—he was writing the *Emergence of the New South* then—of three or four pages he had written on the Scottsboro case.[2] I was immediately hooked. George was not the kind of person who stood over your shoulder all the time. He was very good at sitting down, talking to you about what you were working on, making suggestions. He never tried to dictate topics—he suggested this one at my request—he simply wasn't the kind of person who said that you will work on this. He wasn't a heavy-handed supervisor. Then, once you handed him a draft, he was good at making suggestions. Unless you were really off track, he didn't try to make you write what he wanted you to write, so he was a great advisor. He was also very good at getting back to me. I know how difficult it is. At one time I had seven PhD students, with three or four of them writing chapters simultaneously, and I can remember keeping some of them for two or three weeks, or a month, and feeling incredibly guilty. George never did that. I would hand it into him and a few days later I would get it back, which was always a relief, to know what he thought about things.

How many graduate students have you directed?

Well, in my twenty-six years at Emory, I had over thirty. I don't remember exactly, but it was a lot, thirty-one, or thirty-two. Something like that. It just seems like a lot more.

Do you follow Tindall's model when advising your students?

Well, I don't follow that of my advisor at Wisconsin, William Hesseltine, who was very much an old-school person. He was very intrusive. Wonderful in terms of the writing. He really taught me a lot about it. He spent a lot of time on anything that you turned in to him—literally. Teaching you the mechanics, which I thought that I had down, but it turned out that I didn't nearly as well as I should have. He was very different in that respect. He also was never abusive to me, but he could humiliate students by reminding them how inadequate they were. I may be being unfair to Hesseltine, but I did have him two semesters. He would sometime use weak students as a way of warning others. I wouldn't say that they were pilloried, but they were definitely held up as examples of what not to do. That always seemed odd, because he was a real Virginia gentleman in so many ways. In his seminars, though, he could be merciless. Tindall, on the other hand, wrote his most critical comments, presenting them very tactfully. He would never attack someone in a seminar. He was simply too kind of an individual to ever embarrass or humiliate anybody, and I learned to like that about him.

I think that I try to follow Tindall's model much more that Hesseltine's. There are times when you need to take students aside and suggest that they think about not continuing beyond a master's, but never tell them in a public situation or a seminar. I do think that sometimes you're doing a student a disservice if they really aren't capable of doing good work. They may have the enthusiasm and the desire but just are not suited for it. On several occasions I have told students that, always being careful to couch it in terms that this is my opinion and I may be wrong. There are at least three or four students to whom I said that. But, by and large, I feel that students, both undergraduate and graduate students, respond to positive suggestion much more than the negative. Find their strengths and build on those rather than end up talking about the problems they have all the time. I think that I've never forgotten how vulnerable you feel as a graduate student, particularly during the first year or two. You're always insecure; you're always on the edge, wondering if you're performing well. You are on quite a tightrope the whole time, and the last thing that you need is to be embarrassed or humiliated by a teacher. I just don't think that it is a good teaching model at all. It does mean that you have to be willing to make clear your expectations, but that's a quite different thing from treating students in a way that I think is demeaning.

So, your advice is to simply be honest with them?

Yes. That is a fundamental thing—that you do have to be honest with students about their abilities and where they need to work to improve. Not to do so is a real disservice, especially when you consider the time and money involved in attending graduate school.

Do you have any recommendations for anyone who is considering becoming a graduate student?

Yeah, it's probably not a good idea. I don't do the Doomsday thing. There was a period during the 1970s and 1980s when I would literally sit students down and tell them that they needed to be a little deranged to want to do this and that they needed to think very seriously about it and recognize that there was a very good possibility that they might not be able to make it. Not because they weren't good but because the profession was in such a situation that there are not many jobs. I still warn students about that. But I also don't want to tell people who are really passionate, committed, and capable that they shouldn't do it. Those are the very people we need in the profession right now, and I'm worrying that we are losing some really first-rate people who look at it and say that I can do something else even though this is really what I want to do. So I try to be honest with people about it but also encourage good undergraduates to come into the field.

You say the 1970s and 1980s were the dark decades for employment. What was your job search experience like? How long did it take you to get your first job?

I'm always hesitant to even talk about this because it is so bizarre. I got my PhD during the summer of 1967, and it had been pretty obvious, at least in my mind, that I was going to be through when I went on the job market the previous fall. I interviewed at the Southern Historical Association and the American Historical Association, and by the end of January, I had four job offers. This was the last golden moment—1967 and 1968. You had that big buildup during the 1960s when higher education went through that explosion when the graduate schools ramped up due to a tremendous demand for faculty. You were just beginning to turn out that flood of PhD graduates. So I came along and had all these job offers. I had been offered a three-year instructorship at Harvard and an assistant professorship at the University of Maryland. At the time, I was very interested in the Harvard thing, but they offered almost no fringe benefits, and my wife was pregnant. I just couldn't see living in Boston on a salary that was even less than I was making at College Park. I think the department chairman at Harvard was totally flummoxed. He could not imagine—he even said so—that I turned him down. They had never offered a job—any job—to anyone who wasn't from Berkeley, the University of Chicago, or one of the Ivy Leagues. So for me to turn him down was a quite a shock.

Anyway, I ended up going to Maryland, which was partly related to David Shannon—whom I had taken a course from at Wisconsin—being the head of the department. It was a great department and a great place to be. I loved Maryland. It was a wonderful experience.

What was your course load?

Three. It wasn't bad. I usually taught two sections of US survey and one other upper-level course. My second year I taught a graduate course—it was terrifying. I was totally unprepared at the age of twenty-eight to be teaching a graduate course—half my class was older than I was. I remember thinking that it was not a good idea, but David wanted me to do it. I think that I survived it, but I don't think that is generally a good idea. I feel that you need to teach a few years before you do graduate courses. I have never felt as comfortable—at least for the first eight or nine years that I taught—in graduate courses as I did in undergraduate courses. I found it a much more difficult process than when teaching undergraduates. There is something about the seminar, particularly a reading seminar, that I have always found challenging. Research seminars were always fine—I was always good at sitting down with papers, reading, and making suggestions. But in a seminar where you are discussing books, I think that, deep down, I was always uneasy about what I felt like was the only way to approach it: to engage in a kind of critical analysis of the readings that meant describing how bad they were, how weak they were, or the problems that they had, which is the way that we train. The reality, however, is that many of the books that we discuss are often first-rate pieces of scholarship. I could never quite figure out how to teach them in a way that you could talk about not only where they "failed" and their weakness but also their strengths. It is almost like an unnatural act in graduate school to say something positive about what you are reading. Yet I think that it is important, so I have always tried to do that in my classes, not only to talk about where the book "failed" or where it fits in with the historiography but to say something positive about each work.

That brings up another point. I am a narrative historian. And yet when teaching graduate students the whole emphasis revolves around interpretation. So you end up focusing on books that I don't think are always great models for what students should be reading because it is much easier to discuss a book that is thesis laden or contains a strongly expressed theoretical point of view. They are not necessarily the best work. I go back and look at some of the books that I taught in the 1970s that are totally forgotten today because they were so caught up in a kind of particular theoretical framework of the moment that ten years later they were bypassed—I understand that whole process. History, like the other social sciences, is very competitive, with dozens of people competing all the time. You end up trying to make a name for yourself the only way that you can, coming up with a distinctive point of view or thesis. I try to warn students about that, letting them know not to get caught up in a theory that oftentimes turns out to be nothing more than a fad. And I don't believe this nineteenth-century notion that you have to have a subject totally different from everybody else.

Just concentrate on doing the best job that you can, and things will sort themselves out, even if somebody else is doing the same thing.

Departments doing the hiring for tenure-track positions have aleays valued publishing over classroom performance. Do you still think that is still the case and, if so, how do you feel about publishing being rated as the benchmark over teaching ability?

I think that it really depends on the institution. There are institutions that clearly value teaching over publishing. Then again, there are institutions that may give lip service to teaching but never really find it all that important. I saw it in a case that I dealt with of a person whom I think was one of the most gifted teachers that I have ever known. Very limited publishing, however, so he was dead in the water. There are other institutions where I think they really do care about teaching. This is not that others don't care about the classroom, but the first thing at many places is that you have to be a major publisher.

I know that it is hard to make judgments about publishing. Like everything else, we tend to make subjective judgments about the quality of publishing, so that you have to have a book in order to be promoted. And I think that it is a mistake to look at it so rigidly when you think about all the historical monographs that are out there—works that were clearly done for the purpose of getting a job, of getting promoted, or whatever. I think there are many times when, for example, publishing a really good article is far more important than writing three or four mediocre books. I really believe that in terms of the profession. And moreover, particularly if you really care about teaching, I think that you ought to be flexible enough to say that there are some individuals whose greatest strength isn't publishing but teaching. These people have a gift for teaching, and they are the kind of people who are not going to change once they get tenure but are going to continue to be gifted even after they are promoted. I do accept the notion that there can be, and often is, a relationship between people who publish and end up being good teachers.

On the other hand, that is not always the case. I think about my own research. Sure, there is a connection—my research has strengthened my own teaching. But a lot of the teaching that I do has nothing to do with my research but is owed to intellectual interests that I have that are broader than my own particular subject matter that I'm writing about. So I think that it is foolish to try to set up some type of template that we have to fit everybody into because all of us have had an extraordinary teacher who changed our lives without being a publishing scholar. I know that I certainly did—I had a faculty member at the University of South Carolina, Florence, Jack Thompson, who was never a publishing scholar but an extraordinarily gifted teacher who had a knack for provoking students to think, challenging you to think in a way that you had never done before. I am sure that of all the people in my own intellectual and professional development to whom I owe the most, he would surely be one of the two or three people most important. Even when you make allowances for the lack of publishing, I think that there is always a sense that someone who is just a teacher is one step down on the academic hierarchy—that they don't have the same kind of prestige. I think about some of my students who teach at small liberal arts colleges with heavy teaching loads, and are passionate teachers, but are incredibly defensive to me as though what they are doing is not that important. I want to say to them that in a lifetime of teaching you are going to have a far more profound impact on individuals than you would have if you publish a mediocre monograph that is read by maybe 208 people, but probably not even that many.

To me, while I do see both sides of it, as a whole, it is a legitimate criticism that we, as a profession, do not place enough emphasis on teaching. And I know how hard it is. To this very day I spend hours preparing for classes. Next semester, for example, I'm teaching a course that I've taught in the past, but I'm simply not happy with it. I've already spent dozens of hours trying to get ready for it to really engage the students in a way that I didn't the first time around. There's no particular economic incentive for me to do that, but I do it because I love to teach. I love the involvement with students. I don't know how you reward those who really care about teaching, but I wish that there was a better way of doing it instead of the present system.

Let's discuss your work. George Wallace's family is notorious for protecting his reputation. Did you, during the course of your research, run across somebody who hindered your access to his records? What was their reaction to you? Did they help you in any way?

Not really, but nobody laid down in front of me either. I didn't get the sense that they put out the word not to talk to me. That might have been hurtful, but I was able to interview most of those involved. There were those close to him, particularly those involved in the later stages of his career, who would not talk to me. And George Jr. wouldn't talk to me, but Peggy, one of his daughters, did. Although I had only one extensive interview with her, it was extraordinarily helpful. Still, I wish that I had been able to interview not only George Jr. but the other children as well. But no, I didn't run into that problem, of them hindering my access. The greatest problem that I had with George Wallace was that he never put anything down on paper. I also didn't get to interview him either as he was working on his own book with somebody else at the time. People have this notion that an interviewer can somehow, by asking the right question, penetrate the defenses and get right to the heart of an issue, but a politician of his stature has his answers so finely honed that there is no such thing as an interview that is going to unlock any great mysteries. That was particularly the case with Wallace. All I could do was to try to talk to people who were around him and try to find out everything that I could about him. They were more concerned when I got ready to do the work with Paul Stekler on the film about Wallace.[3]

That was Settin' the Woods on Fire*?*

Yes. Although Paul was in no way duplicitous—they knew that I was an advisor—I don't think that they realized how closely I was working with him on the film and I told Paul not to emphasize our relationship. They were much more open to him than they had been to me. George Jr., for example, agreed to an extensive interview and Peggy also. I think that really helped the film tremendously. This is one of those things that I have really thought about a lot. There is an old saying that if you are a biographer, you are essentially a betrayer. That's your job. Your job is to ask the tough questions, and that means that if you get close to someone that you often end up betraying them because you end up depicting them in all their dimensions. I didn't try to shade it. I let them know that my views were different from George Wallace's but that I was trying to understand the sort of context in which he lived, and that I certainly was going to try to be fair-minded about it. But I remember when I sat down to inscribe a copy of *Politics of Rage* for Peggy, I remember thinking that she's going to be hurt by this—that this book has to be painful for her if she reads it because, while I tried to be fair, it is a pretty incriminating view of her father and his impact on American politics, Alabama, and southern society. But I still did it—it was what I had to do. It doesn't mean that I don't feel bad about it.

Peggy's a remarkable person. I don't want to imply that we are friends, but my dealings with her and her husband, Mark Kennedy, revealed that these are extraordinary people. The same for George Jr. And if it were not for George Wallace's overwhelming ambition I would have probably felt the same way about him. Almost everybody I ever talked with who knew Wallace said the same thing: were it not for his overpowering ambition, Wallace was the kind of man you would end up, on the whole, saying was a good person. Everybody I talked to spoke about how incredibly charming he could be. He was just a very complicated man who got caught up in his own ambition.

So, at the risk of putting words into your mouth, your recommendation to a graduate student undertaking a similar work—a biography of a living figure—is to be honest with their subject. I guess it really goes back to your earlier point that so much of graduate education revolves around attacking—be it pointing out the shortcomings of a book or painting your subject in the worse possible light. I get the sense that you feel the profession needs to remember that gentility is not a bad thing.

Yes. This is something that George Tindall stressed. When I handed him the first draft of the Scottsboro story, it was filled with a certain amount of righteous indignation surrounding it. He said to me, when we met, that my job was not to condemn but to understand. That doesn't mean when you understand that you justify, but unless you are able to understand people, you can't make any judgment about them. That means that you have to be willing—again, not to sympathize with them but to empathize with them, at least to the extent that you can understand—to get inside of their skin a little bit, presenting your story not as a moral tribune but as a person whose job it is, first and foremost, to understand what makes people tick, why they do certain things.

I still think implicitly no matter what I write, I'm still basically that boy who got baptized in Lynch's Creek and wants to make moral judgments, but I try, at the same time, to temper that with the realization that it's easy to make those judgments unless you've been there and seen what those people went through. I've often said that one of the things that anybody should realize before starting out as a historian, writing about people, is that they are people, even if you disagree with them. Somebody like Wallace, for example. People talk about how critical I was of Wallace, yet what I came away with was the deep sense of sadness that surrounded the man. Here was somebody who was incredibly capable and, I think deep down, had a real empathy for people, which made him a very successful politician with the ability to sense people's fears, emotions, and longings. But he allowed those feelings to be overridden by his own ambitions. While many folks see that as despicable, it really makes him, in my mind, a very tragic character as well. Unless you're willing to try to do that as you talk about people, and understand that as you write, then you are just a scold. You don't get anywhere.

Again, I go back to George Tindall and the first chapter that I handed in. It's advice that I remember him giving me after I had spent about a paragraph writing about how awful Scottsboro was. He said, if you describe what happened, and do it well, then readers, if they have any sense of moral sensibility at all, will know that this was a tragedy—they will know this was awful. But if you stand there, beating them over the head, telling how awful this was, then quite the contrary will happen: they will recoil from it and the opposite will happen. So your job is to try to tell it with the fullest understanding of these issues as you can muster. Leave the moral judgment out of it. Although your work may be informed by your moral views—we all have them—it is not your job to tell the reader what they are supposed to think about it. And I have never forgotten that.

That is good advice. One more thing: after spending forty years in southern history, how do you view the future? What I'm really interested in is both the validity of southern history, given that America is becoming more homogenized, and the simple fact that many of those coming into the field are not native southerners. Is this a hindrance, or how do you see these developments?

It doesn't matter. It really doesn't. People have been saying that southern history has been disappearing for more than one hundred years. My own sense is that it is receding as a field much more slowly than people think that it is. Southernness, however you describe it, will continue for a long, long time. It's pretty resistant to even the lure of mass popular culture and television. We know, for example, that linguists used to say that once television became popular that regional accents were going to disappear. Well, that hasn't happened. The same thing is true about southern history—some version of it is going to be around at least until my son retires, and he's in his late thirties. It is certainly changing. The southern history of the 1930s, that of Fletcher Green and the first generation of professional southern historians, was quite different from the work of the postwar generation, like George Tindall who came of age during the 1940s and early 1950s. That was quite different from my generation. It is totally different from that of today, but there is still something in the regional distinctiveness of this country that enriches our way of looking at our nation's history that will be around for at least another generation. It just runs too deep to go away anytime soon.

There's an exercise that I do. On the very first day in my classes on southern history at South Carolina, I ask my students, "How many of y'all grew up on a farm?" Out of the thirty-five or so present, only a few will raise their hands. Then I ask, "How many of your parents grew up on a farm?" That gets about a third of the class to raise their hands. Then I ask about their grandparents, and how many of those lived on the farm. Virtually everybody then raises their hand. What I'm trying to get them to see is that our rural heritage runs deep, far too deep to go away anytime soon. As long as we can keep saying that, then there will always be southern history.

NOTE

1. Charles W. Joyner, *Down by the Riverside: A South Carolina Slave Community* (Urbana: University of Illinois Press, 1984).

2. George Brown Tindall, *The Emergence of the New South, 1913–1945* (Baton Rouge: Louisiana State University Press, 1967).

3. Daniel McCabe and Paul Stekler, *Settin' the Woods on Fire* (Alexandria, VA: Public Broadcasting System Home Video, 2006), DVD. This documentary, part of PBS's *American Experience* series, was partly based on Carter's book *The Politics of Rage: George Wallace, the Origins of the New Conservatism, and the Transformation of American Politics.*

8

From the Bottom Up

A Conversation with Theodore Rosengarten

Charles Kenneth Roberts

Theodore Rosengarten received his undergraduate degree from Amherst College in 1966 and a PhD from Harvard in 1976. His dissertation and first book, *All God's Dangers: The Life of Nate Shaw* (Knopf, 1974), which won the National Book Award (1975), introduced historians of the American South to oral history. Rosengarten's next project, *Tombee: Portrait of a Cotton Planter* (Morrow, 1986), the annotated diary and biography of a South Carolina cotton planter, continued to use an individual to study society.

Through the years, he has worked closely with his wife, Dale Rosengarten, PhD, an award-winning curator of the Jewish Heritage Collection at the College of Charleston. Together they have produced volumes on the African origins of an American art, sweetgrass basketry, and the history of the Jewish experience in the American South. Currently Rosengarten teaches courses in American and modern European history at the University of South Carolina and the College of Charleston, where he is the Zucker/Goldberg Chair for Holocaust Studies.

In February 2010, Rosengarten visited the University of Alabama for a lecture with Dr. Shirley Dean Ray, granddaughter of Ned Cobb, which was sponsored by the Frances S. Summersell Center for the Study of the South. Conducted shortly after the lecture, this interview includes discussions of Rosengarten's studies of tenant farmers and cotton planters, of oral history, and of life in the American South.

Let's start with your undergraduate experiences at Amherst.

Amherst had the first, and an absolutely wonderful, American Studies program, in which students were taught to read literature but with a very strong grounding in history. And to study history meant looking into what one teacher called "the whole articulated culture." Examining all kinds of evidence, studying a little bit of law, music, philosophy, history, all wrapped into the broader picture of American development.

That was a great program; it was a very popular major, and our teachers were terrific historians. They used a debate method of teaching, so that many classes would have two professors who would take different views on a subject. For example, on the removal of the Cherokee Indians, I can remember two professors, I don't remember their names, but I can remember them debating very passionately their points of view. It was an exciting example of what one could do with the presentation of history.

Is that when you decided you wanted to study history?

Actually, I don't know if I decided I wanted to study history then. I knew I wanted to continue in what is called American Studies, studying history, but also our literature, and being as broad based, as eclectic as possible.

What about your graduate school experience at Harvard?

Well, it was a great experience, and not only because of the curriculum. At Harvard, the highfalutin name for American Studies is History of American Civilization, but you could put together your own program, crossing disciplines. So I ended up doing about a third of my work at Harvard Law School studying American constitutional history and labor history, another third of my work was in literature—not just American literature but world literature—and a third of my work was in traditional history courses. And I'll add another third, a fourth third—I did a lot of auditing at Harvard.

I audited history classes simply to hear great professors. And so I was very fortunate to take classes with people whose names you might not know, but should, such as Bernard Bailyn and John Womack, people who were unusually good teachers, but I wasn't enrolled in the classes; I was there as an auditor. I was more interested in how they did their history than in a particular subject.

How did you find out about Ned Cobb?

My girlfriend at the time, who is my wife today, Dale, was a senior studying social studies, and she had to write a dissertation to graduate. She was choosing at the time among subjects. And for various reasons—mostly curiosity, because we had not gone south in the mid-1960s when many friends of ours had traveled to Selma in the march in 1964 and worked in voter registration drives in Mississippi—we wanted to go south and see what we had missed.

Dale was looking at the possibility of studying a defunct agricultural union in Alabama called the Sharecroppers Union. She had a number of leads and felt that this episode of labor organizing in the Deep South could be the subject of a really interesting history. So we went to Alabama together at Christmastime in 1968. And she had been given the name of a survivor of the union, Ned Cobb, by a friend, John Beecher—a Beecher from the old Beecher family, Harriet Beecher Stowe, going way back. He lived in Massachusetts and was a poet, and an older man, and he had written a poem many years earlier about Ned Cobb and the shootout in Reeltown that Ned was involved in, his local branch of the union and the local sheriffs in 1931.

Beecher in fact knew Cobb's whereabouts; he didn't know his exact address but knew he was living in East Tallassee, Alabama. He told us, "Go ask people if you want to find this man." So we came down to Alabama, we worked for a week, Dale scoured records in the courthouse in Dadeville, in newspaper morgues in Birmingham, and Montgomery, and Anniston, and then we went to find Ned Cobb.

What was he like? Cobb comes across in* All God's Dangers *as this larger-than-life, heroic character—what was it like interviewing him?

He came across in real life as somehow larger than average, too. A heroic bearing, and mentally and physically fit. I describe in the preface to *All God's Dangers* meeting him the first day, driving up to his cabin. He lived on a dirt road, and his house was set back quite a bit from the road. That morning he was standing on what he called the veranda of his house, and he looked out at us. We were really nervous; it was early in the morning, and we had not experienced the warmest of welcomes in other places.

Ned looked out at us, and he raised his right hand and said, "I always recognize my people when I see them, children. Come on in, come on in." All the nervousness that we had of being in a new place and not knowing, not having a good foothold, just melted away. And Dale, without much in the way of preliminaries, sat down at the fireplace and asked Ned Cobb one question. She asked him why he joined the Sharecroppers Union, and he spoke for eight hours without stopping.

When we got up we were shaking. We had never been in the presence of someone with such a command of the English language. So we knew, and we knew that other people knew, that this was a very special person.

How did you decide to do a dissertation on Ned Cobb?

When I presented the idea of recording Ned Cobb's life story to my department as the basis of a doctoral dissertation, they said no. They said, "Well, this isn't history, this is the raw stuff of history, you have to do much more with it."

I was very fortunate. My advisor was Frank Friedel, a very important historian of Franklin Roosevelt. He had faith in me, had faith in the idea, and he said, "Leave school and do it." So I left—I officially left school and was not enrolled any longer, and went to Alabama and did the work. It was three years later when the work was transcribed and had become a book that I was called by a dean of the Graduate School at Harvard. He said they wanted to offer me a PhD for my work, and I was thrilled.

I have all the respect in the world for why they originally said what they did, and of course I was very happy how it came out. So I never submitted a dissertation in those black binders. There was the book, and the book got the PhD.

You mentioned when you went back to see Ned Cobb that you had a list of questions for him.

I was a diligent student and had put together—once I had decided that I was going to come down and interview Ned Cobb—a large notebook of questions that dealt with cotton farming, sharecropping, tenancy, whatever I felt I needed to learn about African American life in the rural South, churches and local politics, even national politics to see how clued in he was, questions about all facets of everyday life. I had assembled the questions really from deconstructing other oral histories. If I had to say I had a single important model, it was the work of anthropologist Oscar Lewis, who put together in the 1960s two enormous and wonderful oral histories of Mexican extended families, *Children of Sanchez* and *Pedro Martinez*.[1] I was hoping to use them as models for what I might do with Ned Cobb and his family: Ned, his brothers, and all of his children and their children. It seemed to me that their story followed the journey of a prototypical African American family: roots in Alabama, branches after migration all over the eastern United States.

That's what you expected to do?

That's what I hoped to do, and set out to do.

You mentioned that they didn't seem to think that your dissertation project was real.

That's a good word.

They didn't seem to think it counted as history, and then of course it had this enormous impact on southern history and oral history.

Yes.

So what kind of impact do you think your work has had on southern history or on history in general, and on the recognition of oral history?

To start, I think we all know that what was missing from southern history, and not only from southern history, from the histories of any regions or places, are histories from the bottom up. That is, histories from the point of view of working people who generally don't have access to the means of keeping accounts of daily life and who aren't living their lives so that people at some later date can come back and study them.

All God's Dangers showed that there is a wealth of material, waiting for the collector to come along, that can in fact be the basis for the kinds of history that people with training in archives and reading texts can use to tell a comprehensive story of society or put together a picture of that society that had been missing before.

In Ned's case, Ned had that picture as well. In other words, he wasn't only telling about his day-to-day activities, but he had a view of his place in history, in the history of Alabama, and in the history of black southerners.

But as far as the impact of that work—one of my favorite books and also, in some way, a model for what I've done is called *Conversations with Ogotemmêli*.[2] It's by French anthropologist Marcel Griaule, who lived with the Dogon people in Mali for many years before World War II and after, doing a standard anthropology, collecting as much material as he could about how these people live and what they thought. *Conversations with Ogotemmêli* consists of thirty conversations Griaule had with the village elder before leaving for Europe. He says in the introduction that this book will forever change the idea Westerners have about the mentality of Africans. So I thought, "Oh, that's wonderful. But did it?" Of course it didn't, but it did for him.

And for me, my sense was, "Well, this book *All God's Dangers* should change the way all people think about the mental lives of African American farmers in the American South," to see the perspective people had on their own lives, plus what enormously good record keepers, mental record keepers they were as well. Did the book have that impact? Probably not. But has it played a part in the great development in American history toward freedom, toward freedom for all peoples, toward freedom in particularly for African Americans? Yes, I believe it has.

It's a great pleasure to come back to the University of Alabama now. The first time I was here, in the late 1960s, it was a very, very different place. I mean, the first time I came here was just five years after Vivian Malone and James Hood were admitted to Alabama. Alabama is not only a piece of the world, but by accepting the past without making excuses for itself, the university and the state itself have become world leaders. I would love to think that *All God's Dangers* was a part of that process.

One thing that strikes me about it is the book came out just a couple years before Ned Cobb died, right?

The book came out after Ned died. The book was completed, the manuscript was completed, and he saw the manuscript. I actually got to read parts of it to him. He died shortly after that.

Okay. So in a sense, you were the last shot at getting this incredible story?

I was the last shot. I was also in a way of speaking the first shot, and what I mean is that nobody in his family or outside of his family had attempted to put down his history. He was recognized by people in his community as the historian of the community as well. In many families, I hear over and over again people say, "Oh, I wish I had recorded my grandfather. I wish I had recorded so and so." That's, I think, a very common regret—mine, too. Here I worked with Ned Cobb but I never worked with my grandfather, my mother's father, who escaped the czar and lived to build an empire of kosher delicatessens in New York and who had an amazing history.

Do you feel like we're missing stories like Ned Cobb's right now?

Oh, we're missing them, and they're all around us, but of course, history—the process of writing history—is the process of selection. We have Ned Cobb's story, there are clearly other people who were farmers, who were miners, who were steel workers, if you think back to the people who built Alabama's wealth, whose life histories have not been recorded. They are out there, but let's face it, this is 2010, these are very different days, and those people of the past who are yet with us may not realize that we need their stories.

When I drive through Tallapoosa County today, I see much of the beautiful old farmland is underwater; it's in Lake Martin. Many of the myriad styles of rural architecture, things that we look at and call those old cabins, which represent really many different architectural and social traditions, are gone. They're in firewood, they've rotted, they've gone, they're down, replaced all too often by trailers or abandoned to the weeds. The people are gone, too, many of them are gone.

But still, oral history is a tool, for example, for recording the great period of change in the South, the period of the 1940s, 1950s, 1960s; it's an invaluable tool. I don't think we can get the history of the postwar—World War II—era that was the beginning of the end of the old regime without it.

Right now I'm working on a project [about events] that happened before my lifetime, but during the lives of people I know, and I get this sense of an incredible gulf between myself and the people of the 1930s, this idea that I can't really understand what's going on in these people's lives. Oral history is how we overcome that.

I think that's a fantastic view, that oral history gives us—obviously there's a certain directness about it. But doing oral history is not easy. First finding and identifying the subject, then recording and transcribing, editing and often writing explanatory notes, and organizing the material in a book, at last making it accessible to other people.

When I was doing research for a later work I did on Sea Island cotton, I discovered that not many people know what Sea Island cotton is—the long-staple cotton that was its own industry, as different in its methods of production and marketing from short-staple or inland cotton as short-staple cotton is from rice. To understand the cotton markets in England, you needed to know how the famine in Ireland affected the price of cotton in South Carolina, and how that in turn affected an African American community, whether that community would be enlarged or broken up because England was paying so much less or more for the cotton, because it had to feed these starving people in Ireland. But they didn't do a very good job of that did they?

Okay, the fellow who is hoeing and chopping and picking the cotton doesn't know what's going on over there. But for the historian, one of us privileged folks who has access to archives and to other sources of information, the workers' oral evidence, what the farmer knows about prices on the ground and how he plays the local markets, gives us what we need to understand the period. Though no one source or method can give it all.

To go back to Ned Cobb, do you still keep up with his family?

I keep up with some people in his family for sure; it's a very big family. I'm close to several people, and to others not so close. There has been some resentment from some individuals from the start, people who want to know, why did it take this outsider to come in and do this? Why didn't we get this, why didn't we do it ourselves? Why did it take a white man to come here talking to our dad, to our grandfather?

But most people in the family have been very open to the work, very proud of the work, very proud of it. They are not historians, they're not academics, and so what to me or to you may be a wonderful history is to them granddaddy hanging out the family laundry for people to see. Some are okay with that and some are not.

What kind of reception did you get in Tallapoosa, then and now?

First of all, the part of the family that migrated out of Alabama received the book with the most warmth and excitement. The part of the family still in Alabama were upset in general that their father Ned had talked about people who were still alive. For example, the banker, with whom the family had done its business all their lives, and who still was advancing them money, was a character with a very large role in *All God's Dangers*. When the book came out he was still living and still banking in Notasulga, Alabama, forty years after the events that landed Ned Cobb in jail and so the family certainly didn't want to offend him.

People I had lived with and stayed with, particularly in Dadeville, were thrilled with it. People like the Oliver family—a lawyer, John Oliver, a man who walked out of a Harper Lee novel, whose wife and children Dale and I became very close to over the years—were thrilled with it. While I was doing the work, I'll say again, I had a wonderful time living and working there. People were extremely warm to me, people whose politics were very different than mine and whose social ideas did not coincide with mine. One thing, just a small example: when I got to Tallapoosa, I started coaching a team of ten-year-olds in the Dixie Youth League. The Dixie Youth League, you may remember, was formed when the Little League ordered its franchises to integrate in 1954. And people in the segregated South refused, and so they started this all-white baseball league for boys called the Dixie Youth League. By the late 1960s it was integrated, too, and I got to coach a team in Dadeville, a team that was mixed black and white. I felt that people respected what I was doing, no matter who they were and who I was, because I really had a way of getting those boys around the bases.

I was then, and am now, a devout fisherman, and the fellow who used to sell me the batteries for my tape recorders at the hardware store in East Tallassee went fishing with me, introduced me to his favorite fishing holes, though clearly I did not share his views on race. Perhaps I should not be so sure that we were so far apart. I had a close time with people. I don't know what these different individuals, how they felt when the book came out. Obviously the book shined a spotlight on the community, but not necessarily a negative one.

I do know, for example, that the elementary school in Camp Hill, Alabama, went on to have kind of its own little oral history project, and people came and recorded music from the area that had incorporated some elements of the Sharecropper Union history into songs. So that was terrific. *All God's Dangers* had inspired other people to come into the same area and do more work.

The Cobb family, all of Ned's children, were exceedingly polite to me. But once the book came out, I think some people were just sorry that dad or granddad had said as much as he'd said.

Right. "Why didn't you speak to someone else's granddad?"

Or, "Why didn't you let me speak, too?" In the book, Ned tells a story, for example, about a dispute he has with one of his children. Of course, it's his point of view, and so the child, who is past sixty years old, reads this in the book and says, "Wait a minute, it didn't happen like that."

I said, "I understand that, but that's what your dad said."

"But I didn't have a chance to tell you my side."

That happens. That's the nature of oral testimony. You try to confirm, but the testimony of any individual is going to be one-sided. The first lesson of doing oral histories is that the lives that people want to talk about are their own, and that's what Ned wanted to talk about. And each of his children, when I talked to them, even though I might have come to them to get more information about their father Ned Cobb, or their uncle Ned Cobb, what they really wanted to talk about—and this is one of the real joys and responsibilities of doing oral history—is themselves, which is something they have not done and do not do in the normal course of their lives.

You mentioned the protests in the South, and there were student protests going on at the same time that you were working on this. I heard that you hurt a knee in student unrest of some kind?

[*Laughs.*] Yes, that was in Cambridge, Massachusetts. A group of students at Harvard University was very unhappy about university investment policies and university complicity in the war in Vietnam. And there was a takeover of one of the main administration buildings. I had my oral exams coming up for my PhD, and I wasn't going to get stuck in that. So I stood outside the building watching what was going on and I look around me and behind me and I see there's a long line of police with shields and clubs and I'm in a group of people who are standing between the building and the police and I didn't get out, I didn't get away fast enough.

I was hit, I was hurt. But it wasn't in the role of a protestor. I just wanted to get the hell out of there.

You wrote a biography of this kind of heroic Ned Cobb, and you go from that and you work on a project on Thomas B. Chaplin, who is a less inspiring figure. Did that affect how you approached writing about him?

It is different, but I'm going to come back to the heroism of Ned Cobb and get to Thomas B. Chaplin in a moment. Ned was heroic. He did stand up against injustice. He did feel the weight of oppression, of generations of oppression on his shoulders, but he stood up also for very personal reasons. He stood up because he wanted finally to make a break between himself and his father, from an image of his father, Brown Cobb, whom he'd been wrestling with for many, many years. He wanted to show that he was a man who stood up and didn't slink away from challenges as his father did.

He wanted also to win back the affection of his wife, whom he had alienated through his materialism and his striving, the doggedness with which he went after making a living. Here's a man who owned two automobiles by 1932. What American, never mind black American, never mind a tenant farmer, owned two cars? But in order to get that, he stood accused in his own mind of neglecting another side of his life.

And the third thing, beside the struggle with his father and the struggle with his wife, he wanted desperately to keep his children around him on the farm and knew that he had to preserve and build up his holdings, his possessions, so that his sons would want to stay. It was already too late, he didn't understand that.

So he was heroic, without a doubt, but he was also moved by the same kinds of considerations that move other people.

And then years later—not so many years later, say it was five years, six years after *All God's Dangers* was published—Dale and I were living in South Carolina. We had moved there about a year after the book came out and our graduate community was breaking up with people going off in all directions. We decided to move south because we'd had very good experiences in Alabama and Tennessee as well, and we chose this area on the coast of South Carolina thinking we'd spend a year. That was thirty-four years ago, and we're still there.

I was working in the South Carolina Historical Society, an extensive and wonderful archive in Charleston, and one day the archivist showed me an old volume he thought might interest me. The leather-bound and ledger-size book was a diary. It was written by a plantation owner named Thomas B. Chaplin, who had grown long-staple cotton on St. Helena Island, one of the Sea Islands that would become known for their distinctive African American culture. Chaplin made a record of his everyday life from 1845 to 1861. After the Civil War, by which time he had lost everything he had owned except the diary, he went back and annotated it. So, in reading his diary, I thought, "Oh, this is a wonderful book." It had a beginning and an ending and the author had some literary pretension. I thought

I could write an introduction, annotate it, and put it out there, quick. Eight years later . . .

Tombee gives the reader an in-depth look at the Sea Island cotton industry. It solidifies the case for viewing long-staple cotton as the fifth great staple crop of the Old South. We have the South of cotton, the short-staple upland variety, we have the South of rice, and sugar, and tobacco, and here is the South of Sea Island cotton, which is little known and was an entirely separate industry from the cotton that Ned Cobb was growing a half century later.

Chaplin himself was not a great thinker. He was not someone who reflected deeply on what he was doing. But in this way, he was very transparent. He was like a pane of glass. You get a clear view of society through him, a view of the Sea Island cotton world, and a portrait of a hidden domain of American slavery.

And though he was not a terribly sympathetic man, it's interesting that in his relationships with his slaves, at no point does he indicate that he felt that these people were somehow humanly inferior to him. He believed he had inherited his situation and that they had inherited theirs but not through something inherent in either of them. It was an accident of history that found the black people here and the white people there. Literally, at no point does he feel that he's more intelligent, or that he's more righteous, or that he's a better human being than the people who are working in his fields.

So I found that I could hang with him, I could be there and learn from his diary and take from it this unique picture. The work gave me an opportunity to write about the Sea Island cotton industry and to say something about the horrific banality of racial slavery. Chaplin's own attitude toward slavery really dates to the eighteenth century, not the nineteenth. Though he is ready to defend his property to the death, his grounds are economic and cultural, a defense of wealth and privilege and a way of life without all the philosophical and anthropological reasons used over the years to defend slavery—he had none of that.

There's also a terrific family drama in the Chaplin records. Thomas B. Chaplin's mother, Isabella, on the eve of the Civil War, was one of the richest women in the United States. She owned many plantations. She had married four times, each time acquiring more land and more slaves. Her fourth husband, however, was a bankrupt pharmacist from Charleston who was Chaplin's age, in other words, the age of the woman's son. So you have the son and his stepfather fighting for two decades over the wealth and affections of his mother.

But then the war comes, 1861, washing away the old dramas and bringing new ones. Chaplin lives in that part of the South where the planters lose everything. They lose their land. They lose their slaves. They lose their personal possessions. It doesn't happen anywhere else in the South.

In South Carolina, we say that the American Revolution was our Civil War, and the Civil War was our Revolution. And it was a revolution in the sense of what happened to land and who came to own it. So this story was also embedded in the Chaplin work, and we have a record of it because, in a display of heroism, Chaplin guarded the retreat of the planters off of St. Helena Island in December 1861 when the Union Navy bombarded and invaded Port Royal. Immediately he lost everything he had, left everything, but he returned, snuck back onto the island, got into his old house—he'd left the key with a trusted slave—found his diary and left with it.

And over the years, from 1865 through his death in 1890, he went back and annotated his diary. He didn't write new entries but he would write across the old entries and describe the fates of the characters and how they ended up. Chaplin did not know it, but he was creating a literary form, the annotated diary. And I wanted to work with that text—and to describe a unique social history.

One response to *Tombee* was, "Well, Rosengarten's been living in the South too long. He wrote about Ned Cobb, an African American tenant farmer struggling to save his land and his dignity, now he's writing about a planter." Well, yes. Let's talk about all sides of society. And furthermore, let's develop what anthropologist Clifford Geertz has called a "thick description" of society. That was my goal in working with Ned Cobb. That was my goal in working with Thomas B. Chaplin, too. My motivations were similar.

You've got a sharecropper and a planter, and then you work on this history of southern Jewish life, and African American art—you've worked on a large variety of projects.

Yes.

Do you think that working on such different projects gave you any advantages or insights into the next thing you do?

I think there's a question beneath the question. It's, hey, what's your field? You're doing this. You're doing that. You're doing a little of everything. My abiding interest is in race and race relations. It has been so since I was a kid growing up in Brooklyn, New York, in the late 1940s, and early 1950s, three blocks from Ebbets Field where the old Dodgers played baseball and where Jackie Robinson was integrating America. It was the most exciting time, and I was aware of race, and I knew very early on that I wanted to write, and that race would be a subject of mine, in one form or another.

To be interested in African American history, it behooves you to know something about Africa, to know something about the social origins of these people who would become Americans, where they came from and what they did. Dale, who is a remarkable curator, has put together a show called *Grass Roots: African Origins of an American Art* that compares the coiled grass baskets made by African Americans in coastal South Carolina to baskets made in Africa.[3] It's a gorgeous show.

The book is great.

Yes, the book is beautiful, and it's also very smart. Like the exhibition, it tries to convey how a culture that is traumatized and fragmented and brought to America reconstitutes itself and how we can see that, even hundreds of years later in the living tradition of coiled basketry. The tradition survived the Middle Passage and thrived on Lowcountry rice plantations where baskets were essential tools in processing the harvest. So, yes, I have been to Africa and studied African history, and I find it incredibly useful in understanding developments in America.

My current work, for the last ten years, has been teaching courses about the Holocaust at the University of South Carolina and the College of Charleston. And while this may seem like a leap away from African American history, the history of the Jewish people was an interest of mine from the very first days, growing up in Brooklyn in a Jewish community where many people, all of us, had lost family in Europe during World War II, during the Holocaust, although we didn't have that word, "Holocaust," and as a child I knew many survivors living in our midst. Only we didn't call them survivors, we called them refugees or, speaking impolitely, "refs."

Recently I gave a talk at Chapel Hill called "The Holocaust and the Spirit of Colonialism." And I said, what happens if we take a look at German policy and behavior in southwest Africa in 1900 and German policy and behavior in Ukraine in 1942, what do we see? And people, I have to tell you, were on the edge of their seats. And this isn't anything—the connection of the Holocaust and colonialism—that originated with me. It was in fact a foundational idea of Melville Herskovits, the great American thinker and historian whose major accomplishment was to demonstrate that the African past was substantial and not forgotten, and that African Americans have a history that predates their bondage on this continent.

So I had been looking, in fact, very closely—and not only me because my work is always built on the work of other people—at how the Holocaust fits in a long line of Western colonial genocides, population die-offs, whatever. So to connect—I'll give you one little example. In 1942, when Heinrich Himmler wanted to set up cotton estates in Ukraine for the benefit of the SS, he brought in the Togo Cotton Company to plan and manage them. What is this? What do we see? The Togo Cotton Company had been active in the German colony of Togo in West Africa in the first part of the twentieth century and here it shows up again in Ukraine forty years later.

The Brownshirts, the Storm Troopers, you know where the brown shirts come from?

I do not.

There's no reason to [*laughs*]. At the end of World War I, Germany had lost its African colonies as part of its losses, and the brown shirts were the shirts that the German militia in southwest Africa were typically issued.

So instead, they end up —

They come home?

—they come home and they're worn by the Nazi SA. But those are just some anecdotal parallels. There are also deep parallels in racial thinking and racial policy between what Germans, and certainly not only the Germans, were doing in Africa and what happens in Europe during the Nazi domination.

Do I find that surprising? Well, I didn't think of it, I didn't know this was going to happen, that my interests in Africa, in African American history, and my interest in the Jewish catastrophe would come together—this coming week I'll be teaching about the Nuremberg Laws, which were laws passed by Nazi Germany in 1935 to deprive Jews of their civil rights and their status as German citizens. We'll be looking at those side by side with segregation laws in the American South. Because Hitler told the governors of the German states that if you want to know how to keep Jews and Germans separate, read the Jim Crow laws of the South.

To someone who says, "Well, you've got these interests and they're quite separate. How can you do one and do the other?" I say, as a historian, you've got certain tools and training to look at ideas, to look at how those ideas played into policy and shaped people's experiences. There isn't such a gap as you might see between the work I did with Ned Cobb and Thomas B. Chaplin, or between work juxtaposing the Holocaust and African and African American history.

Do you feel like the field has become too specialized, that people are focusing too much on one very narrow piece of ground?

No, because I benefit from specialization. For example, I have a friend who's researching African American life in one community in western North Carolina. We don't often think of black people settling in western North Carolina, and he's very focused in this area. I'm really happy he's doing that. Now, I'm not doing it, and it's not something that I would do, but I think that, again, our larger picture of the American past will benefit tremendously from people doing the kind of monograph he's doing.

Some historians might consider that these people focus narrowly. But the kind of persistence it takes to do a project—you will learn, I'm sure, if you haven't already, that every book that you write, God, if you knew at the beginning what it would take to complete it, if you knew what it was going to involve, you probably would never have done it. I'm glad people follow their passions. If narrowness is another word for focus, I think the focus benefits all people in the field. I have never felt that a theme is too small or too localized. Not a bit.

You really haven't followed the traditional academic career path. How do you feel that that has affected your research, your teaching?

I've been very fortunate, unbelievably fortunate. When *All God's Dangers* came out, I was still a kid, just out of graduate school. I made a little money and I do mean little, but I thought, "Whoa, this could be a stake. I could go read and write and do my next book." I've always been teaching as well, but I just haven't had a full-time academic job. Not because I was making royalties—I wasn't—but because I could make my living through my writing, make my living editing. I've done that.

How has it affected teaching and what I teach? I think my students will tell you, I'm very focused on what I do. My questions to them—whether in courses on the Holocaust or southern environmental history or agricultural history—are rigorous and very much source based. So I do a lot of reading, I try to keep up with the literature and debates in several fields. It helps that I don't have a regular teaching load. I don't have the responsibilities of committees and the obligations that come with full membership in an academic community.

I haven't wasted my time. I've used my time, but basically for reading and study, and for community activism. The community we landed in, McClellanville, South Carolina, is a place from another century. But some of the same forces that have made it an environmental wilderness have left it socially backward as well. So we had to help build the schools for our children to go to school, build the cultural centers to have the kinds of activities we want where we are.

In the last fifteen years, Dale and I have become more like city people living in the country, and more of our work lives have been centered at the College of Charleston and the University of South Carolina. But for the first period, say 1976 through the early 1990s, it was very much community based. We were fortunate to live in a community with literate people, for whom books matter; but another part of the community has needed change, the kind of change that comes about through social activism. This means if our kids were going to get any kind of an education in the local schools, everyone else's kids would have to as well. So our efforts have been in keeping with our earliest feelings and thoughts about race and human equality.

For students, the graduate students and the undergraduates reading this, do you have any advice to take from your career so far?

You know, I thought that the advice that Shirley Ray [a granddaughter of Ned Cobb] gave yesterday in our talk about Ned Cobb's daughters was really, really good. I want to pass it on. Don't fear, and be passionate about what you do. Don't do something just to get your union card, if the union card is a degree or whatever. But I recognize from watching my own two sons make it in the world, that you guys—how old are you now?

Twenty-seven.

Twenty-seven, you're exactly between my two boys, twenty-five and thirty. In some way, the options you have are much greater than the options and tools we had, but the stresses today seem greater, too. For example, I could go to Alabama with an old jalopy and four hundred dollars in my pocket and live for three months and do my work. You can't do that now. The costs of living and the expectations on you are much greater. It seems to me harder to be a freelancer. I certainly don't advise anyone to do that, but I do advise—in the work that you do—to be passionate and fearless about it, and also to realize that this field that we're in, this field of history, is wide open. It's a perpetual frontier.

For every area of study, sharecropping and tenancy in Alabama, for example, there is still work to do, books are still there to be written. Enough people will be there reading books. Whatever you do, twenty years from now or thirty years from now, you'll be telling the next person it's still to be done.

Just as society has always been dynamic, our field of history is dynamic as well, and the questions that we ask about an earlier time and the people who lived then are not the same questions that people will ask in the future. As long as there is this infinite well of questions there's tremendous work to be done. One thing we have to become better at doing is sharing our passion for history with people outside the schools and the profession. It's not enough to say that we can't know who we are or where we're going without knowing what has come before. Better to live a life of searching that is demonstrably fulfilling and intrinsically its own reward. The great historians I have had the pleasure of meeting and observing were animated each in his or her own way by knowing that the past lives in us and through us and keeps throwing out clues about its nature.

NOTES

1. Oscar Lewis, *The Children of Sanchez: Autobiography of a Mexican Family* (New York: Random House, 1961) and *Pedro Martinez: A Mexican Peasant and His Family* (New York: Random House, 1964).

2. Marcel Griaule, *Conversations with Ogotemmêli* (London: Oxford University Press, 1965).

3. Dale Rosengarten, *Grass Roots: African Origins of an American Art* (Long Island City: Museum for African Art, New York, 2008).

9

Clicking the Trinoculars into Position

A Conversation with Glenda Elizabeth Gilmore

Matthew L. Downs

Glenda Elizabeth Gilmore is the Peter V. and C. Vann Woodward Professor of History, African American Studies, and American Studies at Yale University. Her most recent book, *Defying Dixie: The Radical Roots of Civil Rights, 1919–1950* (W. W. Norton, 2008) recounts the work of civil rights activists during the 1920s, 1930s, and 1940s. Her first book, *Gender and Jim Crow: Women and the Politics of White Supremacy in North Carolina, 1986–1920* (University of North Carolina Press, 1996), won the Frederick

Jackson Turner Award, the James A. Rawley Prize, the Julia Cherry Spruill Prize, and the Heyman Prize. She is a Fellow of the Society of American Historians and has received fellowships from the Guggenheim Foundation, the National Humanities Center, the National Endowment for the Humanities, the Woodrow Wilson Foundation, and the Institute for Advanced Study at Radcliffe at Harvard University. Her current project is *A Homeland of His Imagination: Romare Bearden's Southern Odyssey in Time and Space.*

Born and raised in Greensboro, North Carolina, Gilmore witnessed the civil rights movement firsthand. She earned her BA from Wake Forest University in 1970, and after teaching high school and starting her own business she returned to graduate school, receiving her MA in 1985 from the University of North Carolina, Charlotte, and her PhD from the University of North Carolina at Chapel Hill, in 1992. In this interview, which was originally conducted at the Southern Historical Association's 2008 annual meeting in New Orleans, Gilmore explains how looking through the lenses of race, class, and gender can reshape our understanding of the South.

Let's start with your childhood. Could you tell me what it was like growing up in Greensboro during the sit-in movement?

I was eleven years old when the sit-in movement started. I didn't realize then that I had grown up in a world that was so utterly different from the rest of the country. I think I thought that segregation was everywhere: that it was the natural order of things. My parents were conservatives—they were white supremacists. They believed in segregation, not in a way that they were going to stand up and fight for it, they just were not going to cooperate with any sort of *de*segregation. Fortunately, Greensboro, as William Chafe has told us, is an unusual town. It's a town where a lot of the city's leadership was Jewish. In addition, when I was about nine years old, we moved just outside the city limits to Guilford College, which is a Quaker community. I was in school with a lot of people who were Quakers and extremely liberal, such as children of people who worked for the American Friends Service Committee and of Guilford College professors. That community was a kind of sounding board against which I repeated the things my parents were saying about maintaining segregation. When I would repeat racist things to my friends, or around my friends' parents, or in school, they would all say, sort of gently, as the Quakers do, that they didn't believe in these things. When the sit-ins began I believed that white people were superior human beings. But even at the age of eleven, watching the protests on the local news, I could tell that it was the white people who were being so disruptive. These were not the kind of people that my mother had taught me to associate with. The white guys looked rough and tough, they were wearing jeans and screaming. The black kids were so dressed up and so middle class and so nonviolent. I was probably just at the right age for the nonviolent message to come through. An older white supremacist might have hardened his or her heart against the powerful testimony of nonviolence. But an eleven-year-old girl raised as a white supremacist could tell who the good guys were and the bad guys were at that counter at Woolworth's. The white people were being rude and nasty, and the black people were behaving well.

One of the interesting things about growing up in Greensboro is that everyone thinks that the sit-ins occurred in 1960 and then things ended. But actually there were lots of protests for a long time after that. You often came face-to-face with pickets when you went downtown. They moved from Woolworth's counter, where I loved to eat grilled cheese sandwiches, to the S & W Cafeteria, where I loved to eat strawberry shortcake. When your world is that one small town, and all of its institutions are under incredible pressure, "life changing" is almost too weak a description for what is happening. Everything that I thought was true and forever was under siege. So slowly, not immediately, but slowly, over a period of three or four years, I completely turned around on the issue of segregation by the time I was fourteen.

Two experiences, for me, are really telling about my own transformation. One day I got on the city bus going from my high school, stopping at the gate of Guilford College, and then on to downtown Greensboro. I must have been about thirteen. According to the laws of segregation, white people sat at the front and black people sat in the back. The bus stopped at Guilford College and a white college student—a guy—got on. He looked hard at all of us white folks in the front and walked past and sat in the back with the black people. Everybody on the bus held their breath, all the black people and all the white people. It was the first moment I had seen any white person have any courage about the whole thing. I hadn't seen the white girls from the Women's College when they were sitting-in at Woolworth's; in fact, I don't think I knew about them. So this instance of bus desegregation by the white college boy profoundly affected me. It made me consider for the first time in my life that I had some responsibility for segregation because I went along with its rules. Until then, stupidly (but I was only thirteen), I thought it was something that concerned black people. Then, probably about the same time, maybe a year or two after the sit-ins, I was walking on a downtown sidewalk with my grandmother after watching a parade. I was really flouncing down the street with my nose in the air and coming toward me were two black girls with their arms joined, taking up more than half of the sidewalk. They were about thirteen as well. I looked hard down my nose at these black girls and silently warned them to get out of my way. They didn't, and one of them kicked me in the shin. My grandmother ran. Instead of getting mad at the girls, I suddenly felt the full force of power shift. It became crystal clear to me that they knew that I had been putting on airs of superiority, and just as quickly, I realized I wouldn't get away with that anymore without paying a price. I didn't want to pay a price for white supremacy on the sidewalk. I would just mind my own business. I think that what really hit me was not the kick but that the black girl who kicked me was *just like me*, a smarty-pants teenager who had attitude.

Those kinds of incidents built up until our high school was finally desegregated in 1964. They did it in an ingenious way, and I think they used the same tactic across the South. They got the three best football players from all-black Dudley High School to come to Guilford High School. And that year there were just the three black guys. You might think that would be threatening, given the abundance of us fresh flowers of white womanhood who were sneaking cigarettes in the ladies room, to have three big black football players. In fact, football won. The white guys on the football team so respected these guys, and they were so much better than the white players, that the white players switched their attitudes about segregation. They turned to supporting it and told their girlfriends to do it as well. Of course, the girls dating the football players did everything they said. It was a really interesting move.

How would you say that your own experience in Greensboro affects the way you teach the civil rights movement? Maybe we could also talk about how that experience affects the way you write about the "long civil rights movement."

In fact, I've just written a book, *Defying Dixie: The Radical Roots of Civil Rights, 1919–1950*, about the civil rights movement in the first half of the twentieth century. But I'm pretty careful not to use the word "movement" in that. One way that growing up with those experiences influences my teaching is that I try hard to explain segregation as part of American life. I think it is becoming increasingly hard to convey to students what segregation was actually like, and what an all-encompassing system it was, what oppression was like, what disenfranchisement was like. So in both my teaching and my writing, it is really important to me to be able to be honest about my own experience being brought up as a white supremacist. Our students today tend to think that [exaggerated southern accent] "no one is still alive who opposed civil rights" and *everybody* thought that the "I Have a Dream" speech was a really wonderful moment in American history. We have appropriated and homogenized the meaning of the civil rights movement to imply that only a few crazy racists might ever have opposed it, and, now, we have solved all of the problems that ever existed. It is important to be able to show how normal it was. I can say to my students that I was a racist and so was the overwhelming majority of the seemingly kind white people among whom I lived. White supremacy can be taught, and it might be taught again. Southern white supremacists were not a different kind of people or some vestigial cavemen.

Our students tend to think that segregation was maintained by virulent racists who were a different species of human being. But that is not true. They were also white-haired grannies. Therein lies the danger and the power of this whole thing—that average people can be taught to do almost anything. Human goodness can coexist alongside great evil. People tend to go along in the world within the limits to which they are exposed. That's a really powerful message as far as I am concerned. Growing up in the segregated South—and on the genteel white supremacist side—gives me a way to understand more completely the banality of evil. When I come across something in the archives that seems a little odd, I often remember the odd choreography of the system, all the crazy little conventions of white supremacy, like having to step off the sidewalk if you're a black man.

I remember one time I gave a paper, and I talked about how I was literally taught not to get on an elevator with a black man. If the doors opened and there was a black man in there, I was supposed to just say, "Oh, I'll just get the next one." Or if I was on the elevator and a black man got on and I was the only person on there, I was supposed to pretend that this was my floor and get off. So I gave a talk about this once, and a black man in the audience came up to me and said, "Really? I just really can't imagine that you were taught that. That's just so amazing." I'm sometimes able, because I experienced it, to catch the cues of that choreography in the archives. On the other hand, because I'm a white person who writes about black civil rights, there are things that I don't see from my particular perspective. The gulag of segregation is becoming distant from us . . . like a feudal French village. It's harder and harder to imagine what segregation was like. It's not hard at all to imagine what racism was like—that's certainly survived, that certainly exists—but to imagine the particular configuration of racism in which I grew up is becoming increasingly hard for people, I think.

You mentioned your latest work, Defying Dixie: The Radical Roots of Civil Rights, 1919–1950. *I've heard you call it a "collective biography." Does that help readers connect with the people in the stories?*

Well, any author would hope that the reader would connect with the people in her stories, but the reason I write collective biography is that it helps me connect with the events and arguments. We all come to our work with different questions, but I always ask the same sorts of questions: How did people make the decisions that they made on a daily basis? What was their relationship with power? How did they decide whom they were going to vote for, what they were going to work for, how they were going to claim a full life, a full measure of citizenship? I couldn't answer those questions without having living, breathing people in the book.

Also, I think I've always had this bizarre sense of what historians do. Historians come barreling into history at a certain moment, and they write a book, and they barrel right out, "slicing and dicing" time. People who were living in the Gilded Age didn't wake up and say, "Oh, it's so good to live in the Gilded Age." The time structure is historically imposed. In my writing, I want to be able to slip those bonds. Having characters helps, because I have to tell you how they got there, where they came from, what their connections are to the place and the issues. So I can go back and look at a long arc of time. The full title of this book is *Defying Dixie: The Radical Roots of Civil Rights, 1919–1950*, but with characters, you're able to go back and ask, "How did Lovett Fort-Whiteman's experiences growing up in Dallas, Texas (in the 1890s) lead him to become the first American-born black communist in the 1920s?" With characters, you can move your time periods backward and forward. You can think generationally. At the beginning of the book, for instance, I go back and pick up Fort-Whiteman's dad, Moses, who's coming out of slavery. So I can talk about what it was like to be what they called a "radical black family" on the frontier. The other end of the book is supposed to be 1950, but Pauli Murray goes on to be ordained as the first black female priest in the Episcopal Church in the 1970s. Lives overlap historiographical time periods.

Even as I want to write history as people lived it, I don't want to be confined by one person's life because often that person can't carry the narrative to the times and places it needs to go. I write collective biography, sort of like "six degrees of separation." I have a core of characters and I start adding characters, people who come into those people's lives, and people who are involved in ways that I think are going to help me make arguments. I always begin with more characters than I can actually confine in the space that I will have. I have about ten main characters in *Defying Dixie*. Some of the reviewers reduced it to a book about Lovett Fort-Whiteman or Pauli Murray, but it is just as much a book about Max Yergan and Angelo Herndon and Frank Porter Graham. They all share in this story. In the beginning, I didn't know whom I would follow. You start with a few main characters; then you build a group around them. Writing about African American activists before the civil rights movement means that most of those people knew each other. They were friends and colleagues, so it is possible to re-create the world in which they lived and try to reconstruct the influences on them.

So you go from the individual to building the network, which in turn builds the story.

That's right.

That's really interesting. You mentioned earlier that you went back to graduate school. One of the things I'd like to talk about is your nontraditional path to history. How did you go from a secondary school teacher to graduate school?

It was actually more circuitous than that. I graduated from college and found myself living in Beaufort, South Carolina. I was married to a captain in the Marine Corps during Vietnam and I got a job teaching high school. It was the first year of integration for that school system: 1970! The author Pat Conroy had left this history class and gone out to teach on Daufuskie Island. He later wrote a book about that. My own students were tracked into two shifts by the school district, so I taught from 7:15 in the morning until 1:00. Then a whole other school came in. They were using the formerly white high school because they had condemned the formerly black high school. I was twenty-one years old when I began teaching, and for someone who ten years before had been a complete segregationist, it was a profound immersion in the realities of managing a new situation of integration. Almost all of my students were black at this school, and I knew absolutely nothing about African American history. Nothing. So I taught there for three years, then moved to North Carolina. Teaching in Beaufort had been such an amazing experience that I wanted to put it aside for a while. I didn't think that I could ever be so attached to students again. I had majored in psychology and had worked in personnel, so I began working in what we today call "human resources." First I worked for the Eckerd Drugs chain, which was headquartered in Charlotte, and then for Barclays Bank, which bought a bank in Charlotte. There I managed a pretty large section of the human resources department. I did a lot of management training, so there was still a lot of teaching involved. Teaching adults is really a good thing, really a fun thing. I decided that I wanted more freedom, so in 1981 I opened my own company with another woman. It was a temporary agency; we were sort of the feminist alternative to Kelly Girl—I think they now call it Kelly Services. We did a lot of business with the two banks that are now Bank of America and Wells Fargo. After about five years of working and running this successful company, I gained enough financial independence and time to be able to go back to school. I went to the University of North Carolina [in] Charlotte to get a master's degree in history because I was interested in what was going on in Latin America in the mid-1980s. I couldn't actually be admitted because I had never taken the GRE. So I took a couple of courses and then I took the GRE. I had not had a math class for about twenty years so there were a lot of hurdles. UNC Charlotte was a really wonderful place. Most state universities, even some private universities, admit what they call "special students." You can take two or three courses without having to do anything other than show up and pay for the courses. That is what I did at first before I officially entered the MA program. There were some great professors there—Paul Escott and David Goldfield and Julia Blackwelder.

I began to realize that if I was serious, I couldn't really read Spanish well enough to continue in Latin American history, so I began to pursue my personal interest in southern history. I had been brought up largely by my grandmother, who was born in 1887 in western North Carolina, and I spent a time with two great-grandmothers who were born during Reconstruction in Chatham County, North Carolina. All three lived well into my college years. My great-grandmothers lived to be almost a hundred years old, all the while very coherent. All three talked about the past all the time, and their stories had always been with me. I always thought I knew more about everyday life, the kind of history in which I was interested, than my professors did. When I went to Wake Forest in 1966, history courses were about presidents and elections, and there really wasn't social history. So by the time I showed up at UNC Charlotte twenty years later in the mid-1980s, social history replicated my two great-grandmothers' and my grandmother's stories of the nineteenth-century South. So it was a very interesting time. I wrote my master's thesis on the white rural people who joined the Populist Party in North Carolina and what the Democratic Party had to do to take power back away from it. I had grown up on those stories. My maternal grandmother's family and my paternal great-grandmothers' families had all been Populists. One of the first things that I memorized in my life, when I was probably three or four, was William Jennings Bryan's "Cross of Gold" speech.

So history sort of went ahead, and I waited for it, and we both ended up in the same place in the late 1980s. One day in the hall at UNC Charlotte, David Goldfield said, "You should get a PhD" And I thought [in a naive voice] "Who, me, get a PhD?" I think it's really important that professors encourage students to think of themselves in ways that they might not otherwise. I was thirty-seven or thirty-eight at the time, and I thought that would be a silly thing to do, to get a PhD. But I began to realize that I was going to be forty-two whether or not I got a PhD, so I decided to do it. I was able to commute to Chapel Hill from Charlotte, and I had a great group of professors there and ended up writing a dissertation that I didn't even realize was about my master's thesis from UNC Charlotte.

I had written that master's thesis on white Populists and their enemies, and I thought that my dissertation was on African American people in North Carolina in the 1890s. But I began to realize that it was the same story, a story about political power. So in writing the story that became *Gender and Jim Crow*, I wrote about those same white Democrats who had spoiled the Populists and disenfranchised African Americans.

So you would encourage students who have had other careers to come back to history.

I absolutely would. One of the reasons I was able to do it was that I could use local resources, a great state university system. I didn't have to move. I could continue to work part-time in Charlotte, even when I was a TA in Chapel Hill. I would encourage people to think about this journey in incremental steps. Not to think, "Well, if I can't get into the University of Chicago, my life is over." If you are an older student, start where you are. If you are really interested in history, doing the work is its own reward—and if it is not, the appreciation of others for your work helps as well.

You've touched on it, but I would be really interested in your philosophy as a teacher and writer, and how you approach mentoring graduate students.

I really didn't have graduate students until I went to Yale in 1995. I taught at Queens University in Charlotte for two years—one of my Queens students is a graduate student now at Yale. I've come to see teaching as requiring a lot of different skill sets, some of which I'm better at than others (you know, we're not all equally adept at everything we do). I think that a deep commitment to the historical material is the single most important thing, whether you're teaching undergraduates or graduate students. I think that I have been very lucky to be able to choose my courses at Yale. I don't have a set curriculum or teach certain books. So that luxury is really a blessing—it requires you to continually reinvent your courses and reinvent yourself. One of the most difficult things I had to learn there was to give very polished lectures. In our lecture courses at Yale, there is a performance tradition. So I don't have a lot of interaction with the undergrads in my large lecture course, US Society and Politics, 1900–1945. I give a polished lecture twice a week, but I do go to their sections, so I get to know them that way.

I often teach a freshman seminar in African American history; these classes are the most rewarding ones I've ever taught, in part because they're freshmen, and in part because we plunge right into the Beinecke Library and the James Weldon Johnson collection. Within three weeks of the time that these kids get to Yale, they're holding letters from Langston Hughes in their hands. They're so excited. I turn a lot of pre-med majors into history majors. Their parents are sometimes not happy. At Yale, we also have a senior essay, which means that we work with five to eight undergraduates for a year to write a primary-source-based senior essay that makes an original contribution to the historical literature. All seniors do it. You start in September, and people come to it with different levels of expertise. Most of them come with a strong commitment, because they knew when they became history majors that they would have to do this. It is a fabulous tutorial experience for the professor, different yet again from lecturing and seminars. If you are writing a senior essay, we sit down together in September, and you tell me what you think you're going to write about. Then we spend at least an hour together every other week; I help you get to archives, and I read everything you write. You start writing outlines and drafts, you travel all over the country. Yale has endowments for undergraduates to do historical research!

Let me give you an example. Last year, one of my seniors won the Wrexham Prize for the best essay at Yale. She wrote on the evolution of the Second Line in New Orleans. The Second Line is the jazz funeral parade, not the First Line in a Mardi Gras parade or even in a formal funeral parade, but all the people who follow and dance and play. She traced its development from Africa, which she visited, all the way to the Treme Brass Band. Part of her essay was published in *Southern Cultures*, and another part is coming out in the *Oxford American*. Yesterday I went on my first Second Line for a jazz funeral, all around New Orleans, and we ended up at Tipitina's. I learn so much advising senior essays.

For graduate students, the most important thing to do is to read their work and help them shape their thoughts—my graduate students call me "Edittila the Hun." I approach it knowing that history is not rocket science and that everyone can improve. I try to help them ask the right questions, marshal evidence, and improve their writing. Then I encourage them to find jobs and teaching experiences in which they'll be happy and continue to publish. When I began teaching graduate students, I didn't realize I would be making all of these lifelong friends. Two of my ex–graduate students who are now professors were with me yesterday on the Second Line. Teaching graduate students is a lifelong commitment to continue to read their work. I can't think of a single career that can be so fulfilling in so many different ways, pulling so many different strings together, and I haven't even mentioned that we get paid to read books.

Well, thinking about graduate students, we've talked to several different historians about the prospects for the profession. Some have been optimistic, some have been pessimistic. What is your sense of the future job market for historians?

Your future does not depend on this year's—or even next year's—job market. The job market is bad sometimes, the job market is good sometimes. Right now, it can be very frightening. But almost everyone I know who has stuck with being a historian now has a traditional teaching job. I know one or two people who don't, and that's because they decided to do other things. I think that you should never get nervous about the job market until you have a job offer. It is a total waste of time getting nervous about the job market. It is a total waste of time looking at ads and asking yourself (or, worse yet, your partner), "Would I want to live in Boise?" You don't know if you would want to live in Boise—apply! So the first and most important tip about the job market is *apply for everything*. Present yourself in the best possible way. I gave fourteen papers in graduate school, but I never thought that I was going to be a professor because I thought I could never relocate. Be active in professional organizations. Meet people, get to know people, be truly interested in other people's work. I believe, and I don't think I am going out on a limb here, that after this horrible recession, and within the next ten years, we are going to see an enormous number of retirements and a wave of jobs in history. I understand that many states may react with panic to the current economic crisis and enact hiring freezes in state schools, but I really think that will pass. If it looks like hiring freezes are going to affect you because of the "Second Great Depression," one thing people coming out right now can do is try to buy a couple of years with a postdoc or temporary adjunct teaching positions. Most people aren't as old as I was—forty-two when I went on the job market—so you have more time than you think. Look for postdocs, do more archival work, even work part-time and prolong your student status another year. Try all sorts of short-term ways to get around what might be a tough job market for two or three years. Yale has gone to a tenure-track system recently, in part because it's the right thing to do. But they also know that the current generation of senior historians will soon be retiring at once and bringing junior people along is the opportune thing to do.

That's encouraging. You're one of the few historians we've talked to who has come to prominence during the explosion of race, class, and gender history. Did your path to history help you understand these new movements, or what were then new movements?

Growing up as a southern white girl in the 1950s, critical thinking about the social construction of race and the social construction of gender was at the root of questioning our own existence. We were, of course, told that there were no classes in the South: that we were all nice white people. Until I realized that there were analytically powerful tools of race, class, and gender, I don't think that I began to comprehend the world in which I lived. It wasn't that I was doing the work and "Wow!" all of a sudden I could look at this through a racial lens or through a gendered lens. It was that I was living in the world, and I didn't understand why black people were treated like this. As for gender, frankly, I actually grew up thinking that women were smarter than men, because I came from a home with two women and no men. We were just supposed to hide how smart we were from the men until we married them. So in college, during the feminist movement in the South, I was a very strong feminist, and in the early 1970s, that was what accounted, I'm sure, for my meteoric rise in corporations. They needed women. Experiencing my own life through these lenses helped me use them historically. Being taught mostly lies about what black people wanted and about what kind of privilege white people had made everything foggy until I clicked those binoculars, or trinoculars—race, class, and gender—into position.

But I didn't really experience class in an urban setting until I came to Yale. I understood rural poverty, and I had learned class analysis from Jacqueline Dowd Hall and Nell Painter and Bob Korstad. But living in New Haven, Connecticut, I really came to understand class in the same visceral way that I had come to understand race and gender in the South. It's a great experience to be in a place where there is a proud, multiethnic working class with vigorous politics.

Do you find it easier or harder to write about the South now that you're removed from it?

I think that *Defying Dixie* is really a product of living away from the South. It's about people who tried to change white supremacy, who had been born in the South but who fought it from elsewhere. They were expatriates. They might be living in Moscow, they might be living in New York, some are in Chicago: but they're all southern born and they see themselves as southerners. In *Defying Dixie* I write that I came to see the Harlem Renaissance as the Raleigh, North Carolina, Renaissance North, so many black North Carolinians had moved there. Many of the people in *Defying Dixie* were literally run out of the South because of their politics or because they were black property owners. I came to see this expulsion of brilliant black—and a few white—people not quite as an ethnic cleansing but akin to it. I came to understand that the South is—that region is—a state of mind, it's about where you had your formative experiences, it's about how you came to understand the operations of power. Thus I'm not sure I could have understood how aggrieved my characters felt and how important they felt it was to reclaim their country, the South, if I hadn't been away from it as well. Coincidentally, being away from the South brought me to the fabulous James Weldon Johnson collection in the Beinecke Library. Also I began to travel internationally and came to see global connections among things that I had heretofore seen as uniquely southern.

I'm currently writing about the region where I grew up, and I find it interesting that you have done the same throughout your career. Is that a challenge for you?

I find it amazing. I remember defending my dissertation, and Bill Leuchtenburg, who was on my dissertation committee, asked, "How has this dissertation changed you?" I started talking about what I saw on the drive from Charlotte to Chapel Hill that I never would have known if I had not written that dissertation, even though I had made that drive a million times. It's as if you start lifting the veils and you no longer see the place you thought you knew in the same way. You see different people, you hear different stories, and you understand a configuration of power and hierarchy. You might have experienced or observed parts of that power structure in your own life, but you couldn't have understood the whole of it without understanding its historical construction. Putting it together as a historian is like being the Wizard of Oz. It's like going behind the screen.

Nothing can enrich your life more than a deep understanding of your home. I remember being in the archives in Moscow. It was getting dark at 2:30 in the afternoon, I was freezing, typing in gloves, and I came upon this picture of the communists standing in North Charlotte. They were on a corner before a storefront, holding up signs like "Workers of the World, Unite," "USSR," "Free the Gastonia Prisoners." It was probably 1930. I recognized the storefront to be a place where there is now an art gallery, where Charlotteans now go on Art Crawl to eat cheese cubes and sip wine. It was just like being slapped in the face, to see a place so familiar to me in such an unfamiliar place, with people whom I hadn't known existed standing there telling the workers of the world to unite.

One final question. In the past, you've been fairly outspoken on current events, including the invasion of Iraq. How do you respond to those who argue that historians should only focus on the past?

You know, I was an American citizen a long time before I was a historian. I didn't check my citizenship at the door when I got that PhD. I write about people who participated in political events, and the political events of my time are the events in which I am going to participate. I grew up a lot when I was attacked for criticizing the invasion of Iraq. My mother was watching MSNBC when two conservative Yale students were being interviewed by Joe Scarborough, and they were condemning me for speaking out on Iraq.

The crawl at the bottom was "Traitor Professor," and my mother was just beside herself. It all hurt, at first. Now, I'm so proud of it. Yesterday was the sixth anniversary of the editorial I wrote saying that if we invaded Iraq, it would be a craven abdication of our democratic principles. Actually, I was right. I'm much better able to withstand attacks now, I think. I understand that if you speak up, you have to be willing to take the consequences. But I think it's terrifically unfair, indeed anti-American, that organizations like Campus Watch and David Horowitz's *Front Page News* argued that because I was not a Middle East specialist, I should not speak up about the deployment of American troops or the invasion of Iraq. That is a kind of elitist censorship, and I'm very glad that all kinds of people are speaking up in this election. Liberals and the Left are no longer slow-to-anger, or slow-to-speak-up, when lies are told. They're now calling them into question. I think we live in incredibly interesting times, and I think that it's our obligation—not just our right but our responsibility—to find out what you can find out and to speak up for what you believe to be true.

And do you encourage that in your classroom, with your students?

I do, but I don't ever speak about current politics in the classroom. That's not what I'm there for, and it's not appropriate. I certainly speak about the politics of the time under study. I'm teaching my lecture course 1900–1945, and we are just rolling right into the Great Depression. This year the students are very avid, and we argue all sides of the New Deal. But I try never to reveal in class which party I might be voting for or for whom I might be voting. I do talk about voting rights, I do talk about civics. But when you are the professor, you are not going to convince a student of anything just by pushing your views on them. I think it's an abuse of what little power a teacher has. Students have every right to their political views. If what you teach them about history ultimately shapes their current political views, it's up to them to use the information you have provided as they see fit. I try to create an atmosphere that is capacious enough to make everyone comfortable. Outside of the teacher-student relationship, it's a different story. Then I can be a political person.

Thank you so much for spending your time with us.

Once you start trying to make sense of your life like this, it really is enjoyable. Thank you so much for giving me that opportunity.

10

History without Boundaries

A Conversation with Pete Daniel

Kerry M. Cohen

Pete Daniel's career includes university teaching, working on Capitol Hill, and twenty-seven years as a curator at the Smithsonian's National Museum of American History. He earned his undergraduate and master's degrees from Wake Forest University in 1961 and 1963, respectively, and his PhD from the University of Maryland in 1970. He has published six books, including *Breaking the Land: The Transformation of Cotton, Tobacco, and Rice*

Cultures since 1880 (University of Illinois Press, 1985), *Lost Revolutions: The South in the 1950s* (University of North Carolina Press, 2000), *Toxic Drift: Pesticides and Health in the Post–World War II South* (Louisiana State University Press, 2005), and *Dispossession: Discrimination against African American Farmers in the Age of Civil Rights* (University of North Carolina Press, 2013), and dozens of articles and essays. He is a past recipient of the Herbert Feis Award of the American Historical Association, the Charles S. Sydnor Prize of the Southern Historical Association, and the Elliott Rudwick Prize of the Organization of American Historians. An accomplished historian, Daniel has also served as president of the Agricultural History Society, the Southern Historical Association, the Organization of American Historians, and the Society for History in the Federal Government. After retirement from the Smithsonian in 2010, he began *Dispossession* and other projects.

In this interview, Daniel shares his path to becoming a historian, his graduate school experience, finding his way from academia to public history, and his many other life experiences resulting in a brilliant career.[1]

When did you decide you wanted to study history and why? Did growing up in the South influence your decision to study southern history?

I grew up in Spring Hope, North Carolina, a small town with a population of a thousand. In high school I discovered an aptitude for writing historical term papers. The research, putting parts together, and writing appealed to me. As a kid, I put together complex balsa model airplanes and learned patience and disappointment. As a sophomore I wrote an English assignment describing my first date, a humorous account of misadventures. My English teacher sent it off for a competition, which, she announced, I won. Still, it never occurred to me that I had a special talent for writing, and, indeed, in college English was not my best subject.

When I arrived at Wake Forest College in 1957, it was a small Baptist college that a year earlier had moved from "old" Wake Forest 120 miles to the east in Wake County. Promised support from the Reynolds family, heirs of the R. J. Reynolds Tobacco Company, prompted the move despite Baptist condemnation of the evils of smoking and dire predictions of doom. Baptists furnished a percentage of the operating budget for the college and thus exerted some sin control.

In 1957, the Baptist State Convention banned dancing on campus, a restriction in the age of rock 'n' roll that did not go over well with the student body. During chapel that autumn (we attended two each week, one religious and one secular), alarm clocks went off, and we marched across the lawn (forbidden) to the snack shop in the administration building, rolled the jukebox onto the terrace, and danced. *Life* magazine had a nice photograph of our transgression. It was my first protest; many would follow.

History was the subject that most interested me and that I was best at. The history faculty at Wake Forest included a diverse group of men, no women, and the standard courses for the late 1950s. Thomas Mullen taught me my first college history course, Western Civilization. He had arrived only a year or so earlier and was enthusiastic, approachable, and an excellent teacher. I had a delightful conversation with him in 2011 at my fiftieth class reunion. He was still involved in several notable projects, and I drew him out on his current research. As I was leaving, he smiled and recalled that I was a good student, but he had not expected me to achieve what I have. David Smiley taught southern history and undermined the mythological history that many of us southerners had grown up with. I can still envision Dr. Smiley riding his bicycle to campus with a beret rather than a helmet. He grew up in Mississippi, served in World War II, and did his graduate work at the University of Wisconsin under William Hesseltine. In Germany he found an old man to accompany him around town, and as Smiley pointed to objects, the old man would name them in German. He became fluent. At first I was perplexed by David Smiley's southern history lectures, for he bombarded students with familiar information and unfamiliar interpretations. He also had a patented sneer, sideways smile, unique inflections, and salted his lectures with popular culture asides. I remained in contact with Dr. Smiley, and he gave me a critical reading of the manuscript of *Breaking the Land*. I spoke at his retirement celebration at Wake Forest.

David Smiley fractured the accepted narrative, offering fresh ways of looking at the past. In the 1950s, most white southerners were discouraged from questioning the holiness of the Civil War's Lost Cause, segregation, and the inerrancy of biblical scripture. He challenged conventional wisdom in such a way that disturbed inquisitive students who rushed to the library searching for material to refute him, just what he intended. This was the era when the seminal works of C. Vann Woodward and John Hope Franklin appeared and, along with other revisionist works, inspired fresh interpretations of southern history. The consensus school of writing was ascendant at the time, but history was evolving from a celebratory narrative of facts into increasing analysis and interpretation. It had never occurred to me that I had anything unique to say about the past, but with scholarship so lively I was drawn into debates. Somehow it was always the South that called to me.

I had no plans to pursue graduate school until spring semester registration in 1961, my senior year. I wasn't headed toward an academic career by any stretch. Wake Forest University was starting an MA program in history, and since the better students went off to Harvard and Yale, Wake Forest needed bodies. For Professor Smiley's seminar, I focused on Albion Tourgee, the author, attorney, and northerner who settled in Greensboro during Reconstruction. His legal career intrigued me, and for the first time I delved into legal sources. I wrote my MA thesis on the New Deal tobacco program in North Carolina and later published an article in the *North Carolina Historical Review*. I still recall my elation when I opened the letter accepting the essay for publication. Historical research is sometimes like a sixth sense aided by good archivists and luck. I could tell stories for hours about magically appearing sources, coincidental discoveries, and, of course, the hard work of turning endless pages looking for a gem.

What about your graduate school experience at the University of Maryland?

After earning my MA, I then taught American history at the University of North Carolina, Wilmington for three years. This gave me the opportunity to read widely, including southern fiction, and greatly expand my understanding of history. After three years of teaching, I realized I needed a PhD and entered graduate school at the University of Maryland in 1966.

The location of the school proved fortuitous. I suspected that being near the Library of Congress and the National Archives would be important for research, but I could not have known how important these repositories would be in my career. When I got to Maryland, the formative incident in my graduate education was the arrival of Louis Harlan, who later wrote a two-volume Pulitzer and Bancroft Prize–winning biography of Booker T. Washington and in the second year of my graduate training at Maryland started the *Booker T. Washington Papers*, which was an editorial project. I was the graduate student assigned to that project.

Working on the Washington Papers allowed me to experience a wide range of research opportunities. I traveled to Tuskegee University in Alabama and the Schomburg Center for Research in Black Culture, a research unit of the New York Public Library. Most of my time was spent in the Washington Papers at the Library of Congress and at the National Archives. Booker T. Washington was a political player and a powerful Republican power broker in the late nineteenth and early twentieth centuries. I was sent to the archives to look for these letters. There I explored many record groups searching for Washington letters and in the process met archivists and gained an understanding of government records. When I started my dissertation, it was mostly archival research while at the same time I was working at the Washington Papers, mostly at the Library of Congress, so I was familiar with the Library of Congress and the different holdings there. Through the Washington Papers assignment, I learned documentary editing. Since I was present at the start of the project, I participated in selecting the style and learned the selection, transcription, and annotation process as well as the focus on accuracy. It was especially valuable training to search for annotation information in the stacks of the Library of Congress, now closed to researchers, on obscure African Americans mentioned in Washington's correspondence. I graduated not only with a degree in history but also with on-the-job training in documentary editing. I couldn't have planned it, because I didn't know who Louis Harlan was when I arrived at Maryland. And I didn't really understand how valuable it might be to be near these major archives and libraries.

It was also fortunate that Louis Harlan was friends with August Meier and Elliott Rudwick, two leading scholars of African American history, who were doing research at the Library of Congress in the NAACP Papers. We would eat lunch together, so for me it was much like a seminar. There were other scholars who joined us for lunch, all focused on research projects and eager to talk about history.

I began looking for a dissertation topic and discarded numerous dead ends. One day while reading the NAACP's *Crisis* magazine for the 1920s at the Library of Congress, I came across an article on peonage and then went two floors down to the Manuscript Room and checked the NAACP Papers finding aid and discovered several relevant boxes. Since many of the letters were to or from the Justice Department, I then went to the National Archives where archivist Don Mosholder advised me that there was a very large peonage collection. No one had used it before. He screened out the special agent or FBI reports and brought me several boxes, and I knew after reading several folders that I had a topic. Unfortunately Louis Harlan doubted that peonage would yield a dissertation, and until I turned in several chapters he remained doubtful. I probably spent six months, nearly every day, doing research in the Justice Department records, and more research in the Library of Congress Law Library and other repositories. I still recall going to the desk at the Law Library and asking the staff person where I could find a particular Supreme Court case. I showed him the citation, and he looked over my head and stiffly told me to turn around, go to the section marked federal reports, and then to the cited volume and page, and I would find my case. Mortified but excited, I found my case. This was my graduate introduction to legal research, and I later found that with the same citation I could call up briefs and records. Law review articles were extremely helpful in contextualizing cases and furnishing leads to additional cases and articles.

There were exceptional graduate students at Maryland. Raymond Smock, who later became associate editor of the Washington Papers before serving as the Historian of the House of Representatives and presently as head of the Robert C. Byrd Center for Legislative Studies at Shepherd University, is a close friend whom I met at the history department coffee social in the fall of 1966. David Goldfield, 2013 president of the Southern Historical Association, played poker and Monopoly with Ray, Dennis Burton, and Jim Lane. Donald Ritchie, Historian of the US Senate, came a year later, and Samuel Walker, who worked for the Nuclear Regulatory Administration, wrote important books about the nuclear industry, atomic diplomacy, the Three Mile Island crisis, and Atlantic Coast Conference basketball. Jim Lane has had a remarkable career at Indiana University Northwest. Historians customarily drank at the Rendezvous down on Route 1, and we probably learned more there than in the classroom. Our department softball team won the campus championship, confounding the heavily favored physical education team. In the spring of 1970, Vietnam War protests shut down the university, and we faced a cordon of police on Route 1, a curfew, and drifting tear gas. I had been marching against the war since I arrived on campus and managed to take some good photographs of protesters in downtown Washington. It was an exciting time.

I received my doctorate from the University of Maryland in 1970. After graduation, I received a postdoctoral fellowship at Johns Hopkins University to revise my dissertation for publication, which became *The Shadow of Slavery: Peonage in the South, 1901–1969* (University of Illinois Press, 1972).

During your tenure as a professor at the University of Tennessee, what experiences shaped your teaching style?

The University of Tennessee is a very large state school, and two hundred students attended the introductory history courses. Those were the days of pot and downers, and students tripped over each other and at times seemed on the edge of falling out of their seats. I quipped that my words flowed uninterrupted until they hit the back wall. I also taught African American history, and some of the black students took offense that a white person taught the course. They sniped at me in class and accused me of prejudice, leading to a tense meeting with my critics and the department head. When I walked out of the meeting, a secretary motioned to me and said I had a phone call. A professor at the University of Massachusetts, Boston asked if I would take a one-year position teaching US history and history of the South. I spent the academic year 1974–75 in Boston. Given the tension generated by the civil rights movement and the numbing lessons inherent in African American history about white duplicity, it was not surprising to me that black students objected to white professors. Given my background in the Washington Papers, my research and writing on peonage, and my general disposition toward exploitation, I felt well qualified. Still, a year in Boston proved therapeutic.

Before I returned to Knoxville, I drove through the part of the South affected by the 1927 Mississippi River flood and did research in libraries, interviewed people, copied photographs, and explored the landscape that the flood covered. At some point, I realized that I should change my methodology and focus on oral history and photographs instead of the archival material that I had already collected. Rather than writing a traditional monograph, I explored how to situate oral history and photography on a foundation of archival research. Back in Knoxville I developed the film, printed photographs in my bathroom darkroom, transcribed tapes, and wrote hectically. Part of the motivation was that another book might spring me from Knoxville. Already Ray Smock and I had produced a book on the photographs of Frances Benjamin Johnston, whom Ray discovered while searching for photographs of Booker T. Washington. Johnston had taken photographs both at Tuskegee Institute and at Hampton Institute near the turn of the twentieth century. I still recall finishing the flood manuscript and photographs several days before fall quarter began in 1975 (I also did not like the quarter system) and pouring a glass of bourbon, walking out on my tiny back porch, and looking far beyond the Knoxville skyline from the hill where I lived.

People often ask me why I describe Knoxville as exile. Most important, my young daughters lived in Columbia, Maryland, and I went there as often as possible. I had separated from my wife in 1970. At Tennessee, I had some excellent students and got along well with my colleagues. But I felt that the university was not challenging me, not pushing me to excel, and not particularly mindful of what I was doing intellectually. The town was moribund, the restaurants deplorable, and Big Orange football inescapable. I felt more was demanded of me, and in 1978 when I won a National Endowment for the Humanities fellowship for research and study, I put my worldly goods into a rental truck and headed to Washington with my black cat, Delta Queen. I never went back. Officially I took a leave of absence (for tax purposes) and a year later I was promoted to full professor, several months before I resigned the position.

After Tennessee, you became a curator at the National Museum of American History in Washington, D.C. Was public history always a calling?

After I moved back to Washington, I spent a year doing research primarily at the National Archives looking at documentation for the rural transformation in cotton, tobacco, and rice cultures since 1880. By then I knew many of the archivists, and they invited me to play basketball with them once a week, after which we adjourned to the Keyhole. I rented an apartment near Union Station and continued the annual Broken Heart Ball (a Valentine's Day party, which presently has thirty-six guests) begun in Knoxville, and life was much improved. As the year wound down, a friend invited me to a reception in the US Senate where I met Senator Robert Morgan, a Democrat from North Carolina. He hired me to do oral histories, prepare his papers for the University of North Carolina, Greenville, and ultimately to do aide work and write speeches. The hours were long and the work exhausting, but the ambience of being in the Senate was something special.

After basketball one night, my archivist friends mentioned that the General Services Administration [GSA], which at the time administered the National Archives, had decided to move a large number of records to regional repositories. This would break up coherent series of records and would necessitate that researchers visit several regional branches to trace a topic.

Some records, they told me, were already on skids for the move. Senator Morgan was sympathetic with my effort to halt this move and wrote a letter to the head of the GSA demanding that the transfer be halted pending further study. Later a group of us formed a committee to push for independence for the National Archives, and Senator Morgan introduced an independence bill in 1980. It took several more years for independence to arrive, but the records did not move.

Things were going well until the election of 1980 when Senator Morgan lost to John East, an acolyte of the other North Carolina senator, Jesse

Helms, in the Reagan landslide. In January 1981 I was unemployed. I hold the record for the fastest fall from full professor to unemployed. My career path seemed to be heading off a cliff. I landed a job at the Department of Education, and as that was ending chatted with National Museum of American History curator Gary Kulik at a reception, and he asked if I would be interested in working on an exhibit on the one-hundredth anniversary of Franklin D. Roosevelt's birth. They needed someone who knew documentary photographs. Since I had put together a slide collection on the Farm Security Administration's work the year before on a project with Ray Smock, I was qualified. I worked that summer with Arthur Molella, who had come to [the museum] from the Joseph Henry Papers. Then, miraculously, I got a fellowship to the Woodrow Wilson International Center for Scholars then located in the Smithsonian Castle. In 1956 my junior high school class had gone to Washington, and it never occurred to me then that one day I would have an office in the Castle. I began writing *Breaking the Land*. As that year was winding down, a curator from the American History museum went on leave, and I was asked to replace him. They kept me.

After I began working in the museum world, people would come up to me and commiserate, insisting that someday I would get a real job in a university. That attitude was, and is, persistent among many academicians. They didn't consider the museum work I was doing a real job because I wasn't in the academy. I was learning new things doing museum work and also continuing my historical research and writing. The routine I had in the museum, especially the first fifteen years I was there, was challenging and fulfilling.

I was working on exhibits, collecting objects, and going on quite remarkable research and collecting trips. I was, of course, answering inquiries, being a bureaucrat, attending dull meetings, and doing all those things you have to do. But work was not confining; it wasn't boring freshmen every year and grading papers that testified to failed teaching. Every day was different, different projects, different things to collect, a very challenging job.

How much interaction with the public do you have at the museum? What is the best part about designing exhibits for public display? Is it the chance to research various topics?

Curators have a variety of jobs. People write to or call the Smithsonian requesting, sometimes demanding, answers to numerous and varied questions. I always gave a responsive reply, something I learned working in the

Senate. When people find something unusual, they want to know how valuable it is. Curators cannot give estimates on value but can supply information about the history and importance of objects. Occasionally someone would call or write about a valuable old relic that sat in a nearby field and insist that it should be in the Smithsonian. I always asked for a photograph. Few people sent them. I think that when they actually looked closely at the object (tractor, plow, combine, and so forth) and saw their photograph they understood that it was probably junk. On the other hand, such a call resulted in our collecting a magnificent cotton gin from the early twentieth century. Any number of projects intersected with the public, especially collecting and oral history work.

Exhibit work is unlike writing a history monograph. It is a cooperative enterprise that requires negotiation and compromise. Ideally exhibits spring from curatorial research and go through a process in which curators, specialists, designers, and educators find objects, images, and sounds and create an arrangement that will bring the research to life. Writing exhibit labels is difficult, for one is trying to find the sweet spot that informs museum visitors from eight to eighty, from the uneducated to those with a PhD. An exhibit is more than wall text, illustrations, and objects. These elements work together to create a unique whole that exceeds its parts. The result is a product created by a team. One of my criticisms of current museum exhibits is that too many come not from curatorial research but from funders' desires for a celebratory presentation.

For me exhibit work paid off in my scholarship. Had I not worked on the *Science in American Life* exhibit and its predecessor, *Science, Power, and Conflict*, I would never have written articles and a book on pesticides. Louis Hutchins, who assisted me in research, found files in the National Archives dealing with the fire ant spray campaign of the late 1950s, and later I followed up with more research. The video interviews of rock 'n' roll and soul performers gave me invaluable insight for a chapter in *Lost Revolutions*. An exhibit has a far wider audience than do most history books.

Before we discuss your books, I'd like to return to the notion of celebratory exhibits, which, as you note, aren't really in sync with current historiographic trends. But the public seems to enjoy them. This is a common problem—academics often don't reach an educated lay audience. We see this in the history section at any bookstore, but it seems that museums might amplify this disconnection even more. Do you think we have a responsibility to bridge that gap? And if so, how do we do it? Where do we begin?

Celebratory exhibits are inevitable, for often it is appropriate to commemorate people and/or events. Indeed, the exhibit on the hundredth birthday of Franklin D. Roosevelt offered me an introduction to exhibit work. Not only did I do research in documentary photographs but I also looked at radio transcripts and films of fireside chats and listened to radio speeches by Huey Long and Father Charles Coughlin. This exhibit project led to a conference on the New Deal that included art, drama, photography, radio, and politics. It was a research-driven exhibit. This approach contrasts vividly with what happened when Lawrence Small became Smithsonian secretary at the turn of the twenty-first century and ordered the staff of the National Museum of American History to install an exhibit on the presidency in less than a year so that it could open before the election of 2000. When curators complained that they did not have enough time to conduct serious research, Kenneth Behring, one of the museum's primary donors whose name is now on the building, suggested they use encyclopedias. As a result, the exhibit featured objects connected with the presidency but very little historical grounding that put it in perspective.

I will offer examples of two kinds of celebratory exhibits. The year 1987 was the two-hundredth anniversary of the signing of the US Constitution, and it was the one-hundredth anniversary of the Hatch Act, which established federal experiment stations. Director Roger Kennedy decided that instead of a usual tribute to the Constitution the museum would mount an exhibit on Japanese internment during World War II, focusing on a moment when the Constitution failed. Both Kennedy and curator Tom Crouch received death threats from those who thought this unhappy episode should not be aired, but in the end the exhibit was installed. As visitors approached the entrance with words of the Constitution writ large on the wall, TV journalist John Chancellor explained that this was not a celebratory moment but rather one that furnished a cautionary warning about freedom. There was a paradoxical celebratory section of the exhibit, for Japanese American soldiers who fought in the European theater of the war earned an astonishing number of medals for bravery, fighting for freedom even as their relatives were in concentration camps. This exhibit challenged visitors to think about the Constitution not as a static document but as one imbedded in history.

Representatives from federal experiment stations also asked for their own commemorative anniversary exhibit, and what began as a case-sized exhibit grew into an expensive and overly ambitious treatment of genetic engineering, boldly titled *The Search for Life*. Museum director Kennedy bypassed the usual channels for approval and review and allowed a designer to install a cell theater with dozens of video projections and sound tracks colliding over opaque labels suggesting wonder but generating confusion. The exhibit opened, closed, opened again, and was finally sent away into obscurity. There had been no attempt to complicate the exhibit with some of the controversial issues that were currently generating questions about genetic engineering.

As the museum relied increasingly on Kenneth Behring's funding, his interests pushed exhibit themes. Without going into detail, *The Price of Freedom*, an exhibit funded primarily by Behring on military actions of the United States, received devastating reviews and suffered from treating military success and not raising questions about the larger questions that surround war.

I think that the public is far more receptive to balanced, even controversial, exhibits than museum administrators believe. It is impossible to please every person who walks through an exhibit, but bending to large or small interest groups, as has happened several times with the Smithsonian, demeans curators and robs the public of getting beyond conventional wisdom. The national history museum should be on the cutting edge of exhibit presentation and utilize the latest scholarship. Most people like a challenge, and that is what the Smithsonian should be offering.

The most egregious example of donor intrusion was the $38 million that Katherine Reynolds offered the museum to install a hall of great achievers. No museum curator would have put forward such a topic, but, given the eagerness of Secretary Lawrence Small's administration to court dubious funders and the museum director's acquiescence, it gained traction. Basically, some curators attempted to convert Reynolds's preposterous suggestion into a legitimate historical treatment of achievement. Ultimately Reynolds pulled her money, complaining that the curators simply did not share her ideas about achievement. Interestingly, Wayne Reynolds, Katherine's husband, headed a great achievers organization that gave golden plates to those he deemed worthy recipients. Lawrence Small had chartered a private jet for $18,000 to fly to Texas to receive his plate, an item that later came into play as he resigned in disgrace. Behring, of course, also had a golden plate.

Let's return to your monographs. You have several highly acclaimed works. Does finding topics come easily for you? Several of your books and exhibits deal with the same topics. Does an exhibit lead to a book or does the book direct an exhibit?

How books have developed has always been a mystery. As I mentioned earlier, *The Shadow of Slavery* emerged from reading about peonage in *Crisis* magazine. The flood book grew out of a chapter on peonage in relief camps during the 1927 flood. Exiled in Knoxville, I began thinking about how quickly sharecropping and small farmers declined in Nash County where I grew up. My grandfather Calvin Hunt's shrinking tobacco allotment gave me some insight. I applied for an NEH fellowship based on my primitive understanding of these forces, and as *Breaking the Land* developed my preconceptions about the New Deal and agricultural policy changed drastically.

Lost Revolutions further explored subjects that appeared in an article I wrote on World War II in the South and expanded to include agricultural policy, pesticides, and cultural trends informed by work on exhibits and oral history interviews. When I began, I thought I would write on the South during World War II, but in the postwar years the South experienced drastic tension and transformation as the civil rights movement, rock 'n' roll, cultural changes, chemicals, and mechanization occurred. I don't recall any one thing that pushed me into the 1950s, but I knew by the time *Science in American Life* opened in 1994 and I won a Regents Fellowship for research that this was the target. I learned that although I grew up in the 1950s I knew very little about the historical currents that ran through the decade. It was much like David Smiley's challenging southern sacred cows as I discovered that there was another 1950s. It took intensive research in the National Archives plus visiting repositories throughout the South to uncover the story. The sections on popular culture and civil rights were a departure from my usual concerns.

As I mentioned, *Toxic Drift* grew out of two exhibits that included pesticides. My most recent book, *Dispossession: Discrimination against African American Farmers in the Age of Civil Rights*, further explores discrimination within the US Department of Agriculture and owed little or nothing to my museum work. By this time, my curatorial talents were no longer appreciated by museum leadership, and as much as possible I focused on research. Many historians avoid the National Archives and Records Administration, for government records are voluminous and require patience and persistence. I have spent years going through government records. By the time I gave the first installment of *Dispossession* at the Southern Historical Association convention, I was isolated in the museum and given no creative work. While searching records at the National Archives, I could not find some agricultural records after 1960 and asked archivist Joe Schwartz if any existed. He consulted a few binders, went to the computer, and fifteen minutes later informed me there were 1,145 uncatalogued boxes. These proved invaluable.

When I sent off the final manuscript for *Dispossession*, I thought of a book on wildlife photography, since I had been to Africa on safari a half-dozen times and often bored friends with my photographs and stories. As a kid I was in the Baptist Church's Royal Ambassadors, as I recall a group that met and learned of missionary work abroad. David Livingston, the iconic but, I learned later, largely ineffectual missionary to Africa, loomed large in the lessons. In high school I read the Africa novels of Ernest Hemingway and Robert Ruark and safari stories in *Field and Stream*. In my mind, Africa was exotic and compelling. In the bush, I always kept a journal recording what I saw and comments on the people from all over the world I met in the camps. As I moved through my wildlife photographs and journals constructing a narrative, it occurred to me that my museum career and my work with history organizations might provide context. I tried flashbacks but found them inadequate if not confusing. Finally, I went back to my correspondence files and started reading from when I started at the museum, 1982. All of my adult life I have been a prolific correspondent. I realized how vibrant the museum was then with exciting collecting trips and exhibit work. Even before the numbing *Enola Gay* crisis in the early 1990s and the nonsense about political correctness, I had objected to the increasing power of donors to shape exhibit content and the diminishing power of curators. In my mind, in the early 1990s the Smithsonian lost its nerve after the *Enola Gay* controversy as the secretary ruled that there would be no more controversial exhibits. Curators at the National Air and Space Museum had been preparing an exhibit on strategic bombing, including the atomic bomb dropped on Hiroshima, and an early draft leaked to a military magazine and ignited protest that enveloped Congress and others who accused the museum staff of favoring Japanese at the expense of Americans. Despite a century and a half of conservative exhibitry and a staff that was anything but radical, the Smithsonian secretary seemed to agree with the critics and scrapped the exhibit, hanging the curators out to dry. This resulted in a chill throughout the Smithsonian as curators realized that scholarship must yield to pressure groups. By this time, museums had turned to private funding for exhibits, and the problem of donor intrusion into exhibits increased. The decline of curatorial authority and donor intrusion became extremely important, and I fought in vain to correct this imbalance.

You often examine the South through different lenses than do many historians: agriculture and technology, among other things. How does this avenue enrich our understanding of the South and its culture and, beyond that, the United States as a whole? And, likewise, more and more southern historians are studying the environment—how do you think this will benefit the field?

For the same reason that I insist on exhibits that go beyond conventional wisdom and rely upon cutting-edge historical scholarship, my research and writing have focused on ignored aspects of southern history. Peonage, flood victims, farmers caught in a massive transformation, southerners facing confusing issues in the 1950s, the health effects of pesticides, and discrimination by the US Department of Agriculture deal primarily with poor rural people. I'm not sure if I'm drawn to such topics or if the topics draw me. Fortunately the things that I have written about have been compelling, exciting, and, I hope, important. Writing about characters who do not usually enter the historical narrative has always interested me more than focusing on the usual suspects. Rural life has always fascinated me, something that probably goes back to my grandparents Calvin and Annie Hunt, who raised a family of eleven, none of whom ended up farming.

Environmental history is extremely important, especially when looking at the South. It is not just the eroded land but also the use of chemicals, the hazardous sites left behind by government and industry, and the poor choices for sustainability that have attracted historical scrutiny. As I mentioned, museum exhibits pulled me into environmental questions, and what I found was disturbing. In *Science in American Life*, our research team looked at pesticides, nuclear waste at Hanford, Washington, and health questions surrounding the two atomic underground tests at Tatum Dome in Mississippi. When I was asked to give the Walter Lynwood Fleming Lectures at Louisiana State University, I probed deeper into some of these questions. A telegram in the Agricultural Research Service [ARS] records at the National Archives and Records Administration led me to a Mississippi Supreme Court case, a trial transcript in Jackson, a law office in Drew, and several oral histories on a poisoning case in Sunflower County, Mississippi. It was exciting detective work. The ARS was part of the US Department of Agriculture and until 1970 was responsible for pesticide safety, and its records in the National Archives show frightening malfeasance. By the way, I have used federal records extensively in my work, and although it sometimes takes months plowing through bureaucratic memos and reports, there are gems that are revelatory. The same is true of legal records that historians often neglect. The vast records in the National Archives will not all be digitalized, nor should they be. Archivist Joe Schwartz and I once gazed down rows of ARS records reaching into the distance, and he said that I was the only person who had ever used them.

I hope we can get you to talk a little about today's graduate students and the history profession. What advice would you have for young, future historians currently in graduate school? Is there a special way to prepare for a career in public history?

I had two PhD students at the University of Tennessee, Nan Woodruff and James Burran, and since then nearly all of my contact with graduate students has been through the Smithsonian fellowship program. The Smithsonian awards fellowships for short-term, predoctoral, and postdoctoral research. This is a very competitive program, and fellows are free to focus on their projects. Over the years I have advised dozens of students, both those assigned to me and others who adjourned after the Tuesday colloquiums to the Irish Times. Conversations there have ranged from the banal to the sublime, but there was always an interest in projects, discussion about sources, and helpful suggestions. For me it was a continuing education seminar, for these fellows, pre- and postdoctoral, were at the top of their game. I have three shelves of books written by Smithsonian fellows.

Unfortunately I cannot recommend a route to a career in public history. Mine is certainly no guide. A degree in history is excellent preparation for many positions, for the ability to write and analyze is invaluable. There are public history courses in many departments and even occasionally museum studies. Public history is divided between those who teach courses on the subject and those who work in museums, parks, government agencies, research firms, and congressional staffs. Despite the good pay and satisfying work, many academic historians look down upon those in the public history sector.

I want to reiterate that an academic position is not mandatory for a life of scholarship. Many of my Smithsonian colleagues write important books, give talks throughout the world, work on outstanding exhibits, and appear on TV. The Society for History in the Federal Government [SHFG] is an enthusiastic organization that holds an annual conference, gives awards for books and exhibits, enjoys an annual banquet and a holiday party, and publishes a journal and newsletter. SHFG members were instrumental in the move for independence for the National Archives and for framing a statement on museum exhibit standards. Many historians work at the National Park Service and at the numerous agencies throughout the federal government, both in Washington and throughout the country. Many of these historians perform their day jobs and moonlight writing historical monographs. There are several notable companies that do contract history work for corporations. My friends in public history, whether teaching it or working at it, are carrying history beyond the books that are so important in generating ideas. I believe in history without boundaries.

NOTE

1. The original interview was conducted at the November 2010 annual meeting of the Southern Historical Association in Charlotte, North Carolina. Additional contents were added to this interview by Megan L. Bever in the summer of 2012 and at the November 2012 meeting of the Southern Historical Association in Mobile, Alabama.

Selected Bibliography

Reflections on the Field of Southern History and the Historical Profession

Ayers, Edward L. *What Caused the Civil War?: Reflections on the South and Southern History*. New York: W. W. Norton, 2005.

Bailyn, Bernard. *On the Teaching and Writing of History: Responses to a Series of Questions*. Hanover, NH: Montgomery Endowment, Dartmouth, 1994.

Banner, James M., Jr. *Being a Historian: An Introduction to the Professional World of History*. Cambridge: Cambridge University Press, 2012.

Boles, John B., ed. *Autobiographical Reflections on Southern Religious History*. Athens: University of Georgia Press, 2001.

———. *Shapers of Southern History: Autobiographical Reflections*. Athens: University of Georgia Press, 2004.

Cimbala, Paul A., and Robert F. Himmelberg, eds. *Historians and Race: Autobiography and the Writing of History*. Bloomington: Indiana University Press, 1996.

Du Bois, W. E. B. *The Autobiography of W. E. B. Du Bois: A Soliloquy on Viewing My Life from the Last Decades of Its First Century*. New York: International Publishers, 1868.

———. *Darkwater: Voices from within the Veil*. New York: AMS Press, 1920.

Flynt, Wayne. *Keeping the Faith: Ordinary People, Extraordinary Lives*. Tuscaloosa: University of Alabama Press, 2011.

Franklin, John Hope. *Mirror to America: The Autobiography of John Hope Franklin*. New York: Farrar, Straus and Giroux, 2005.

Inscoe, John C. *Writing the South through the Self: Explorations in Southern Autobiography*. Athens: University of Georgia Press, 2011.

"Interchange: The Practice of History." *Journal of American History* 90 (September 2003): 576–611.

Johnson, Bethany L. "The Southern Historical Association: Seventy-Five Years of History 'in the South' and 'of the South.'" *Journal of Southern History* 76 (August 2010): 655–82.

Kirkendall, Richard S. *The Organization of American Historians and the Writing and Teaching of American History*. New York: Oxford University Press, 2011.

Link, Arthur S., and Rembert W. Patrick. *Writing Southern History: Essays in Historiography in Honor of Fletcher M. Green*. Baton Rouge: Louisiana State University Press, 1965.

Mathews, Joseph J. "The Study of History in the South." *Journal of Southern History* 31 (February 1965): 3–20.

McPherson, James M., and William J. Cooper Jr., eds. *Writing the Civil War: The Quest to Understand*. Columbia: University of South Carolina Press, 1998.

Schulz, Constance B., and Elizabeth Turner, eds. *Clio's Southern Sisters: Interviews with Leaders of the Southern Association for Women Historians*. Columbia: University of Missouri Press, 2004.

Smith, John David, and John C. Inscoe, eds. *Ulrich Bonnell Phillips: A Southern Historian and His Critics*. Athens: University of Georgia Press, 1990.

Stephens, Randall J. "Justifying Slavery in the Old South: An Interview with Lacy K. Ford." *Historically Speaking* 11 (April 2010): 35–36.

———. "Teaching and Writing about the History of African-American Christianity: An Interview with Paul Harvey." *Historically Speaking* 12 (November 2011): 25–26.

Stephenson, Wendell Holmes. *Southern History in the Making: Pioneer Historians of the South*. Baton Rouge: Louisiana State University Press, 1964.

Tindall, George B., ed. *The Pursuit of Southern History: Presidential Addresses of the Southern Historical Association, 1935–1963*. Baton Rouge: Louisiana State University Press, 1964.

White, Deborah Gray, ed. *Telling Histories: Black Women Historians in the Ivory Tower*. Chapel Hill: University of North Carolina Press, 2008.

Woodward, C. Vann. *Thinking Back: The Perils of Writing History*. Baton Rouge: Louisiana State University Press, 1986.

Yerxa, Donald A. "On Slavery and Antislavery: An Interview with David Brion Davis." *Historically Speaking* 8 (July/August 2007): 26–28.

Notable Works on Southern Identity

Burton, Orville Vernon. "The South as 'Other,' the Southerner as Stranger." *Journal of Southern History* 79 (February 2013): 7–50.

Cash, W. J. *The Mind of the South*. New York: A. A. Knopf, 1941.

Cobb, James C. *Away Down South: A History of Southern Identity*. Oxford: Oxford University Press, 2005.

"Forum: Commemorating Seventy-Five Years of the *Journal of Southern History*." *Journal of Southern History* 75 (August 2009): 531–766.

Phillips, U. B. "The Central Theme of Southern History." *American Historical Review* 34 (October 1928): 30–43.

Potter, David M. "The Enigma of the South." *Yale Review* 51 (October 1961): 142–51.

Vandiver, Frank E., ed. *The Idea of the South*. Chapel Hill: University of North Carolina Press, 1974.

Woodward, C. Vann. *The Burden of Southern History*. Baton Rouge: Louisiana State University Press, 1960.

Contributors

Blake Scott Ball is a doctoral candidate at the University of Alabama. His dissertation explores public debates over religion, politics, gender, and policy and the creation of mass media icons in post–World War II America through Charles Schulz's *Peanuts* comic strip.

Megan L. Bever is an assistant professor of history at Missouri Southern State University. Her dissertation, completed at the University of Alabama, explores alcohol, morality, and citizenship in the Civil War era.

Glenn David Brasher earned his PhD and is a history instructor at the University of Alabama. In 2008 he was a finalist for the Southern Historical Association's C. Vann Woodward Award. He is the author of *The Peninsula Campaign and the Necessity of Emancipation: African Americans and the Fight for Freedom.*

Charity R. Carney received her PhD in history from the University of Alabama in December 2009. Her first book, *Ministers and Masters: Methodism, Manhood, and Honor in the Old South*, was published in 2011. Her current project explores the making of the southern megachurch and currently teaches history at Western Governors University.

Kerry M. Cohen is a doctoral candidate in the history department at the University of Alabama. Her dissertation research is on the history of the southern publishing industry prior to and during the Civil War.

Matthew L. Downs received his PhD from the University of Alabama in 2010. He is an assistant professor of history at the University of Mobile.

Michael W. Mansfield graduated from the University of Alabama in 2005. His dissertation, "A Slide, a Swing, and an Oak Tree: Maysville, Alabama, and the Birth of an African-American Community," was recognized as the Outstanding Dissertation by the university's College of Arts and Sciences. He is currently an adjunct instructor at the University of Alabama in the Departments of History and Gender and Race Studies.

Christian McWhirter is an assistant editor for the Papers of Abraham Lincoln, a "long-term project dedicated to identifying, imaging, transcribing, annotating, and publishing all documents written by or to Abraham Lincoln during his entire lifetime." He received his doctorate in history from the University of Alabama in 2009. He published his first book, *Battle Hymns: The Power and Popularity of Music in the Civil War*, in 2012.

Joseph W. Pearson is an assistant professor of history at Union College. His dissertation, completed at the University of Alabama, explores the political culture of the American Whigs, specifically probing the shared underpinnings of their political thought and moral temper across class, gender, and section.

George C. Rable holds the Charles G. Summersell Chair in Southern History at the University of Alabama. He is the author of numerous books, including *Civil Wars: Women and the Crisis of Southern Nationalism*, *Fredericksburg! Fredericksburg!*, and *God's Almost Chosen Peoples: A Religious History of the Civil War.*

Charles Kenneth Roberts received his PhD from the University of Alabama in 2012. His dissertation explores New Deal efforts to alleviate rural poverty.

Scott A. Suarez is a doctoral candidate at the University of Alabama. His dissertation examines the development of the state of Florida as a result of federal defense spending during the first half of the twentieth century.